Writing for Social Studies

W9-AZV-459

McDougal Littell

A HOUGHTON MIFFLIN COMPANY

Evanston, Illinois ▪ Boston ▪ Dallas

With minor exceptions, this book follows the style for documentation set forth in the *MLA Handbook for Writers of Research Papers*. Documentation style for some recent technologies, including on-line computer services, has been updated.

Copyright © by McDougal Littell, a division of Houghton Mifflin Company. All rights reserved.

No part of this work may be reproduced or transmitted in any form or by any means, electronic or mechanical, including photocopying and recording, or by any information storage or retrieval system without prior written permission of McDougal Littell Inc. unless such copying is expressly permitted by federal copyright law. Address inquiries to Manager, Rights and Permissions, McDougal Littell Inc., P.O. Box 1667, Evanston, IL 60204

Printed in the United States of America.

ISBN-13: 978-0-395-86909-3   ISBN-10: 0-395-86909-9

17 18 - crw - 09 08 07

Contents

Writing for Assessment

How can you succeed on a social studies test? Of course, you have to thoroughly understand the material you have studied. Sometimes, however, understanding the concepts isn't enough. To do well on many social studies tests, you must be able to convey your knowledge clearly in writing. This section of *Writing for Social Studies* can help you succeed at test time.

Assessment Types

First, you should identify the type of assessment you are dealing with. The comprehension questions and chapter reviews in your textbooks are one kind of assessment. Tests are another. Tests come in two basic forms: classroom and standardized.

Classroom tests. Classroom tests are those given regularly by your teachers. Like textbook questions and reviews, classroom tests usually require not only objective answers but also longer written responses.

Standardized tests. Standardized tests are those given to students across the country and scored against national norms. Many standardized tests, such as the SAT (Scholastic Assessment Tests) and the ACT (American College Test), require you to analyze social studies readings. As you will see, the same skills that help you to analyze and interpret essay questions can also help you to analyze and interpret these readings. Some standardized achievement tests, such as the CEEB (College Entrance Examination Board) tests for social studies and for history, also include essay sections.

The rest of this chapter looks at the types of questions you are required to answer on many social studies tests.

> "To do well on many social studies tests, you must be able to convey your knowledge clearly in writing."

Questions Based on Graphic Devices

Many social studies tests ask you to interpret or complete graphic devices, such as time lines, tables, graphs, and flow charts. When interpreting such graphics, be sure to note what information the question is asking you to interpret. Sometimes a graphic device includes information that is not necessarily relevant to the questions. This is intended to see if you are able to select the proper data.

Time lines show the order of events, such as historical incidents and discoveries, as well as eras and trends. A time line is divided into segments, each representing a certain span of time. Events are entered in chronological order along the line.

TIME LINE

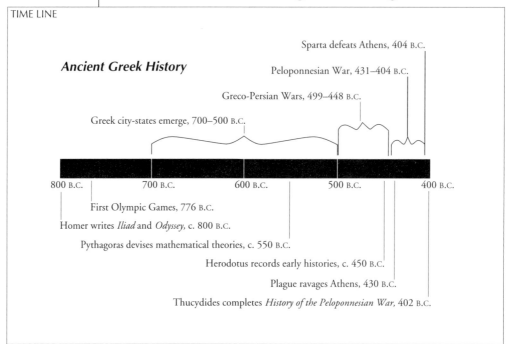

To interpret or complete a time line, take into account not only the dates and order of events but also the types of events listed. You may find that events of one type, such as wars and treaties, appear above the line, while events of another type, such as scientific discoveries or cultural milestones, appear below it.

Tables show numerical data and statistics in labeled rows and columns. The data are called variables because their values can vary.

Average Hours of TV Usage per Day in America
("6.28" denotes 6 hours 28 minutes of viewing.)

	1971	1976	1984	1985	1986	1987
February	6.53	6.49	7.38	7.49	7.48	7.35
July	5.08	5.33	6.26	6.34	6.37	6.32
Year's Average	6.01	6.11	7.08	7.07	7.10	7.10

To interpret or complete a table, read the title to learn its general subject. Then read the column and row labels to determine what the variables in the table represent. Compare data by looking along a row or column. If asked, fill in any missing variables by looking for patterns in the data.

Graphs, like tables, show relationships involving variables. Graphs come in a wide range of formats, including pie graphs, bar graphs, and line graphs.

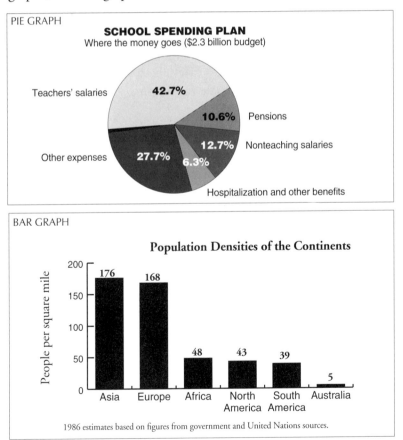

PIE GRAPH

SCHOOL SPENDING PLAN
Where the money goes ($2.3 billion budget)

Teachers' salaries — 42.7%
Pensions — 10.6%
Nonteaching salaries — 12.7%
Hospitalization and other benefits — 6.3%
Other expenses — 27.7%

BAR GRAPH

Population Densities of the Continents

People per square mile

Asia	Europe	Africa	North America	South America	Australia
176	168	48	43	39	5

1986 estimates based on figures from government and United Nations sources.

3

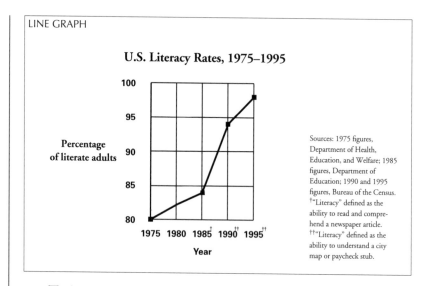

LINE GRAPH

U.S. Literacy Rates, 1975–1995

Percentage of literate adults

100
95
90
85
80

1975 1980 1985[†] 1990[††] 1995[††]

Year

Sources: 1975 figures, Department of Health, Education, and Welfare; 1985 figures, Department of Education; 1990 and 1995 figures, Bureau of the Census. [†]"Literacy" defined as the ability to read and comprehend a newspaper article. [††]"Literacy" defined as the ability to understand a city map or paycheck stub.

To interpret or complete a graph, read the title to find out what the graph shows. Next, read the labels of the graph's axes or sectors to determine what the variables represent. Then notice what changes or relationships the graph shows. If asked, fill in any missing variables.

Some graphs and tables include notes telling the source of the data used. Read these notes carefully. Knowing the source of the data can help you to evaluate the graph.

Web diagrams and related devices, such as cluster and tree diagrams, show relationships between ideas or events. Details, examples, or related incidents are shown on branches extending from a central idea, event, or theme.

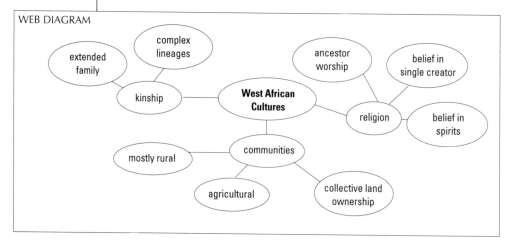

WEB DIAGRAM

complex lineages

extended family

ancestor worship

belief in single creator

kinship

West African Cultures

religion

belief in spirits

mostly rural

communities

agricultural

collective land ownership

4

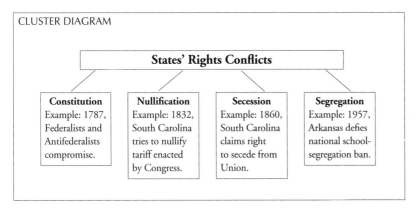

CLUSTER DIAGRAM

States' Rights Conflicts

Constitution
Example: 1787, Federalists and Antifederalists compromise.

Nullification
Example: 1832, South Carolina tries to nullify tariff enacted by Congress.

Secession
Example: 1860, South Carolina claims right to secede from Union.

Segregation
Example: 1957, Arkansas defies national school-segregation ban.

To interpret a web or cluster diagram, first identify the central concept. Then classify the entries that branch out from it. For example, they may give details or examples supporting a general statement, causes or effects of an event, or characteristics of a person, an issue, or a historical period. If asked, complete the diagram by supplying entries in appropriate categories.

Flow charts show processes whose steps include multiple possibilities. To create or interpret a flow chart, you can use the devices described in the Writing Tip at the right or invent similar ones of your own.

Writing Tip

In many flow charts, ovals stand for starting and stopping points; diamonds, for decision points; and rectangles, for possible choices or actions. Arrows show directions of movement.

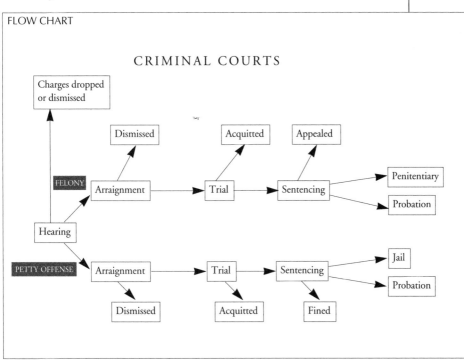

FLOW CHART

CRIMINAL COURTS

5

To interpret a flow chart, read the title and find the starting and stopping points. Follow the arrows to trace the steps in the process. Be sure to note all the possibilities at each decision point, so that you see all possible consequences of each decision.

Developing your ability to interpret graphic devices will help you correctly answer assessment questions based on them. You can also use simple graphic devices to organize and present information in your answers to other questions, as well as to provide facts and data that supplement your answers to short-answer questions and essay questions.

Short-Answer Questions

A short-answer question is one that requires a one- or two-sentence response. Keep in mind the following guidelines for answers to short-answer questions:

• **Use specific names, dates, and figures whenever possible.**

Sample question: What does the "School Spending Plan" graph show about salaries?

Too general: It shows that salaries take up most of the budget.

More specific: It shows that teachers' salaries account for 42.7 percent of the budget and salaries of nonteaching personnel account for 12.7 percent.

• **Respond in complete sentences; avoid sentence fragments.**

Sample question: Why did Cabrillo initially fail to discover San Francisco Bay?

Fragment: Because of fog.

Complete sentence: Cabrillo sailed past San Francisco Bay without seeing it because of a heavy fog.

• **Make your responses brief but thorough. Rely on precise ◦nouns and verbs rather than vague terms.**

Sample question: For what is Ernest Rutherford best known?

Wordy and vague: Rutherford was a person who did many important things in his area of science and made major kinds of advances in learning about atoms.

Brief and precise: Rutherford, a physicist, discovered the structure of the atom.

Whenever possible, respond to short-answer questions before you tackle essay questions. Short-answer questions ask for facts and details; they help you recall some of the specifics you will need in your essay responses.

Essay Questions

Essay questions require longer, more detailed writing than short-answer questions. One secret of success in answering them is efficient planning. Don't just jump into writing. A brief pause to organize your thoughts before you write can pay major dividends when your test is graded.

Budgeting Your Time

Believe it or not, on a timed test the clock is your friend. Look at the total amount of time you have for the essay portion of your test. The average high school student can write half a page in five minutes. Bearing this in mind, estimate how much you will be able to write in the allotted time, and take your estimate into account as you plan your responses. Give yourself a few minutes to quickly analyze each essay question, or **prompt,** and plan a response. In addition, leave yourself several minutes at the end of the test to edit and proofread your responses.

Analyzing Prompts

Key words in essay prompts tell you which writing strategies to use in your responses. The list of strategies and key words on the next page can help you analyze prompts and plan effective responses.

Writing Tip

When you answer an essay question on a test, you may find it helpful to think of the process as a shortened version of the writing process outlined on pages 11–12.

Key Words in Prompt	Tasks	Writing Strategy
explain, discuss, explore	Make an event, a process, a problem, or a relationship clear and understandable. Include examples and reasons.	explanation
identify, show, tell about, what is/are	Explain the distinguishing characteristics of a subject or the meaning of a term. Use specific details.	classification (identification/ description/defini- tion)
compare, contrast, discuss similarities and differences	Show likenesses and dif- ferences. Support your points with details and examples.	classification (comparison and contrast)
analyze, who, causes and effects, examine, show how, explain why, in what way(s)	Show causes and effects, or break a subject down into its parts, showing how they function and relate to the whole. Use facts and examples.	analysis
trace, summarize, outline	Give a condensed descrip- tion of an issue, an event, or a sequence of events. Omit minor details.	summary
evaluate, pros and cons, in your opinion, in your judgment	Present your judgment on an issue, an event, or a historical or political fig- ure. State your criteria, and evaluate the subject on the basis of each.	synthesis (evaluation)
interpret	Consider the significance of a subject in the context of your total knowledge, and explain it in your own words.	interpretation

Planning Your Response

Main points. For an essay response, your planning must be streamlined. Take into account the writing strategy suggested by key words in the prompt, but don't try to make a complete outline or a detailed cluster diagram. Instead, jot down a quick list of the main points your response will cover. Number them in the order in which you plan to discuss them. As a rule of thumb, plan to devote one paragraph to each main point. You might also want to jot down important dates, statistics, and names so that you won't have to grope for them as you write.

It's a good idea to turn in your planning lists along with your response. Even if you don't quite have time to complete your response, your lists may show your instructor that you know the material.

Thesis statement. Write a thesis statement that sums up the essential thrust of your response. Your thesis statement can use words from the prompt, as in the following example:

Prompt: In what ways was Franklin Delano Roosevelt's presidency unique?

Thesis: Franklin Delano Roosevelt's presidency was unique in three main ways.

Or your thesis might be a general, one-sentence answer to the prompt—in effect, a summary of the response you plan to write:

Thesis: Franklin Delano Roosevelt exercised brilliant leadership in dealing with a number of crises that faced the United States.

Keeping your thesis statement in mind as you write can help you shape your writing.

Writing Your Response

Introduction. A one- or two-sentence introduction is fine in an essay response. Your thesis statement can serve as a one-sentence introduction. If your introduction consists of more than one sentence, be sure that one of the sentences states your thesis.

Body. Devote at least one paragraph to each of your main points. Use transitions to show how these points are related to your thesis and to one another. Pack your paragraphs with as many relevant names, dates, and statistics as possible. (In some

"No one expects test responses to be immaculate, but making them legible will earn you the scorer's gratitude."

essay tests, the number of applicable facts and statistics you mention directly affects your score.) If you lose your train of thought midway through your writing, glance at your planning list to get yourself back on track.

Conclusion. As with the introduction, a one- or two-sentence conclusion is fine. This may be a restatement of the thesis in different words. Remember that your conclusion should leave your reader with a clear understanding of your main idea.

Editing Your Response

When taking an essay test, you don't have time to rewrite your work, but you can still edit it. Read your work and check it against your planning lists, to be sure that you have included all relevant information. If you think of things to add, write them neatly in the margins, using arrows to show where they should be inserted. Use arrows, as well, if you want to move sections of a response.

Finally, proofread your responses, correcting errors in spelling and mechanics. Make your corrections as clear as possible: use a single line to cross out each error, and write the correction above the crossed-out material. No one expects test responses to be immaculate, but making them legible will earn you the scorer's gratitude; so proofread neatly, turn in your responses, and congratulate yourself on a job well done.

Completing Classroom Assignments

In social studies classes, you are often required to explore your own thinking in essays, book reports, and reviews. You may also be invited to explore the broad expanse of history by creating primary materials of your own, such as interviews, oral histories, and historical narratives. This section of *Writing for Social Studies* offers guidelines for such written assignments.

Essays

Years ago, the principal meaning of *essay* was "to try." Today, *essay* more commonly refers to a piece of writing that explains facts and ideas. To write an essay is, in a sense, to try out your thinking. When you write an essay, you will go through three main stages—prewriting, drafting, and revising and editing— though these are not steps that you must complete in a set order. You may return to any one at any time.

Prewriting. In the prewriting stage you explore your ideas and discover what to write about. See pages 53–54 for a list of questions to help you choose a topic. Other techniques for finding an essay topic are group brainstorming, freewriting, and making a cluster diagram. When you have selected a topic, note your initial thoughts about it and then do the reading and research you need to understand it.

Drafting. This is the stage at which you put ideas on paper and allow them to develop as you write. Decide on the focus, or thesis, of your essay, then create a list of main points and details that support your thesis. You may find it useful to arrange your material in an outline (see page 72). Carry out any further research you feel is necessary, and then write your first draft.

Revising and editing. In this stage you improve your first draft. The changes you make will usually fall into three categories: revising for ideas, revising for form and language, and proofreading for mistakes in spelling, grammar, usage, and punctuation.

> "You are often required to explore your own thinking in essays, book reports, and reviews."

Some of the changes you make may be inspired by the suggestions and comments of a peer or classmate.

The specific characteristics of essays vary, but most strong essays have the following features:

A focus on one major idea, or thesis. In the opening paragraph, identify the focus of your essay in a way that makes readers want to read on.

Several main points explaining the thesis. In each paragraph of the essay's main section, or body, cover one main point related to your thesis. Start a new paragraph whenever there is a shift in your ideas or emphasis.

Enough specifics to support each main point. Make sure that the specific facts, statistics, and examples in each paragraph support that paragraph's main point.

A clear train of thought. Arrange paragraphs in the most appropriate order, and try to make the links between them clear. One way of doing this is with transitional words such as *on the other hand* and *as a result.*

A conclusion summarizing the main points and the thesis. In the concluding paragraph, tie all of the main points together. You might restate your essay's thesis here.

Essays of Analysis

To **analyze** something is to break it down into its component parts and examine the ways in which the parts are interrelated. You might analyze congressional committees, examining their relationships to one another or to Congress as a whole. You might analyze a primary source, examining how it shows the influences of the time and place in which it was written. You might write a **causal analysis** of a historical event, examining the relationship of the event to its causes or effects.

Planning Essays of Analysis

Make notes of facts, examples, and data that are related to the topic of your analysis. If you are analyzing a parts-to-whole relationship, you might construct a web diagram (as shown on page 4) to help you visualize the relationship. If you are analyzing a primary source, you might list characteristics and examples

Writing Tip

The following are examples of assignments for essays of analysis:

• Analyze the interactions between nationalism, imperialism, and secret alliances in the period before World War I.

• Cite passages of the Declaration of Independence that reflect the experiences of the American colonists, and explain how each influenced the colonists' demands.

• Analyze the causes and effects of the U.S. intervention in the Panamanian revolution of 1903.

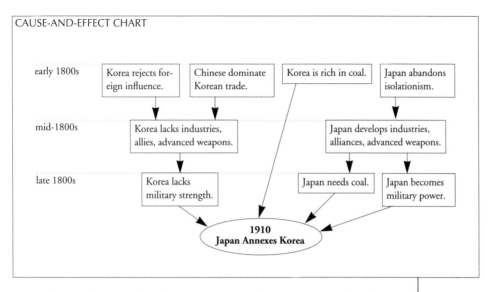

CAUSE-AND-EFFECT CHART

| early 1800s | Korea rejects foreign influence. | Chinese dominate Korean trade. | Korea is rich in coal. | Japan abandons isolationism. |

mid-1800s: Korea lacks industries, allies, advanced weapons. — Japan develops industries, alliances, advanced weapons.

late 1800s: Korea lacks military strength. — Japan needs coal. — Japan becomes military power.

1910
Japan Annexes Korea

in a cluster diagram (as shown on page 5). For a causal analysis, try a cause-and-effect chart.

On the basis of your planning notes and (if applicable) your diagram, write a thesis statement that sums up, in a single sentence, the major idea of your essay.

Sample Thesis (Parts-to-Whole Analysis): Congressional committees accomplish much of the actual work of Congress.

Sample Thesis (Analyzing a Source): Canassatego's "Offer of Help" shows the priorities of Native Americans in the 1700s.

Sample Thesis (Causal Analysis): Some of the effects of the Treaty of Versailles were causes of World War II.

Then list the main points that your analysis will cover. Consider how you might best organize your material. For example, in a causal analysis you might first state a cause and then explain its effects, or you might first explain an effect and then examine its causes. Sometimes you'll want to describe a chain of cause-and-effect relationships. The organization you choose will depend on your topic and purpose for writing.

Writing Essays of Analysis

Introduction. Let readers know what you will analyze and how you will analyze it. Stating your thesis is one way to accomplish this.

13

Body and conclusion. Write a paragraph explaining each of your main points. Use transitional phrases such as *because, as a result, in the first part,* and *in the next part* to make relationships clear to readers. To help readers understand your ideas, include facts, data, and examples from your planning notes. You might conclude with a restatement of your thesis in different words.

Writing Tip

The following are examples of assignments for essays of interpretation:

• What does the information you have read suggest about Chinese attitudes toward children, and what implications might these attitudes have for life in China 20 years from now?

• Present the main arguments for and against the lifting of the United States embargo on Cuba, and discuss the assumptions underlying these arguments.

Revision Checklist

- Have I made relationships clear? Where might I add transitions, facts, or examples for greater clarity?

- Have I avoided oversimplification? For example, have I taken into account multiple causes and effects?

- Are my paragraphs in an order that makes sense? Might any sections of my essay be more effective if I moved them?

Essays of Interpretation

To **interpret** something is to consider its significance in the context of your total knowledge. You might interpret facts or events by writing a **hypothesis**—a guess that you can test—about their implications. You might interpret a primary source by exploring the viewpoint it expresses. You might interpret an issue by presenting the arguments on both sides and examining the assumptions that underlie them.

Planning Essays of Interpretation

If you are writing an essay in which you advance a hypothesis, you might conduct a survey or poll to test your hypothesis. If you are interpreting a primary source, you might fill out a cluster diagram (as shown on page 5) to help you identify viewpoints and find examples. For an argument, you might try a tree diagram.

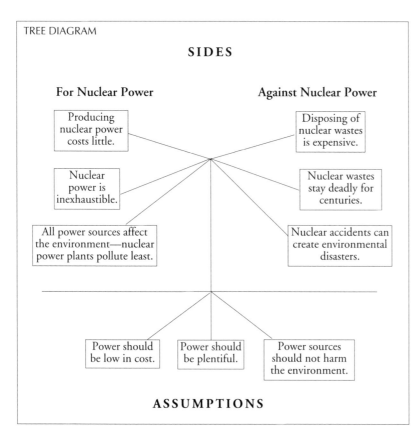

TREE DIAGRAM

SIDES

For Nuclear Power   Against Nuclear Power

Producing nuclear power costs little.

Disposing of nuclear wastes is expensive.

Nuclear power is inexhaustible.

Nuclear wastes stay deadly for centuries.

All power sources affect the environment—nuclear power plants pollute least.

Nuclear accidents can create environmental disasters.

Power should be low in cost.

Power should be plentiful.

Power sources should not harm the environment.

ASSUMPTIONS

On the basis of your planning notes, write a thesis statement expressing the main idea of your interpretation.

Sample Thesis (Hypothesis): The call for welfare reform may imply that Americans fear for their financial futures.

Sample Thesis (Arguments): Both Federalists and Antifederalists assumed that individual rights should be protected.

List the main points that your essay will cover, and then choose the best way to organize your material.

Writing Essays of Interpretation

Introduction. In your opening, identify the source, issue, facts, or events that you will interpret. Then present your thesis.

Body and conclusion. Use the body paragraphs to support your thesis. Include specific data and statistics from your planning notes. If you have advanced a hypothesis, state the facts on which you based your guess and then tell how you tested it. If you are interpreting a source, provide examples to illustrate your points. If you are interpreting arguments, be sure to give equal weight to both sides of the issue. Explain the underlying assumptions on each side, and support your statements with factual evidence or experts' opinions. You might close by noting the significance of your interpretation.

Revision Checklist

- Does my reasoning make sense? Should I take into account other options and possibilities?

- Have I made my reasoning clear to readers? Where might I add transitions to improve clarity?

- Have I included enough evidence? Which points might I strengthen by adding more facts or data?

Essays of Classification

To **classify** things is to sort them according to their characteristics. You might write an essay of **comparison and contrast,** examining the similar and differing features of two concepts, events, or historical figures. You might write an essay of **definition,** explaining the features of a thing or concept so that readers can identify it and understand it.

Planning Essays of Classification

If you are writing an essay of definition, a web diagram (as shown on page 4) can help you categorize your subject's features. To organize your thoughts for an essay of comparison and contrast, try making a Venn diagram. Write similarities in the region where the circles overlap and differences in the nonoverlapping parts of the circles.

Writing Tip

The following are examples of assignments for essays of classification:

• Compare and contrast the various European nations' colonial settlements in North America.

• Define the term *brinkmanship* as it was used during the Cold War. Give examples to illustrate your definition.

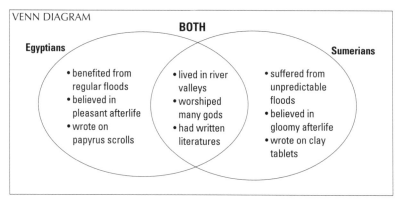

VENN DIAGRAM

BOTH

Egyptians

- benefited from regular floods
- believed in pleasant afterlife
- wrote on papyrus scrolls

- lived in river valleys
- worshiped many gods
- had written literatures

Sumerians

- suffered from unpredictable floods
- believed in gloomy afterlife
- wrote on clay tablets

Write a thesis statement in which you sum up an overall idea suggested by your planning notes. You can then look over your notes or diagram for facts and details that support your thesis.

Writing Essays of Classification

Introduction. Specify what you will compare, contrast, or define.

Body and conclusion. To compare and contrast, you can choose one of two organizing patterns. In an essay organized subject by subject, you first discuss one subject and then discuss the other, pointing out similarities and differences. In an essay organized feature by feature, you address each feature in turn, showing how the subjects resemble or differ from each other in terms of that feature. In either case, keep your readers oriented by using transition words such as *on the one hand, on the other hand, similarly,* and *in contrast.*

Revision Checklist

- Have I made my subject clear at the beginning of the essay?

- What is my organizing pattern? Have I kept it consistent? Have I used transitions to make it clear?

- Have I included enough examples, facts, and data about each feature? Where might more specifics strengthen my essay?

In a definition, present the features of your subject by category. You might devote one paragraph to identifying characteristics, another to uses or effects, and another to background or origin.

You might close your essay of classification with a summary of your points or a restatement of your thesis.

Essays of Synthesis

To **synthesize** ideas is to put them together in your own way. You might synthesize evidence in an essay in which you draw a **conclusion** about a historical event. You might synthesize your thoughts in an essay of **opinion** about a social issue. You might synthesize judgments in an essay explaining your **evaluation** of the solution to a historical, political, or social problem.

Planning Essays of Synthesis

A synthesis often starts with a question, such as "What do I think about this?" or "What do these facts add up to?" When you have chosen a topic, start gathering information. You might make notes based on observations, memories, or research. For a synthesis, the more input, the better. You can't base a valid conclusion, opinion, or evaluation on just a few details.

Try putting into words the question that triggered your synthesis. Then write a one-sentence answer based on your planning notes. That answer can serve as your thesis. List several reasons (again, based on your notes) that support it, and choose the best way to organize your material.

Writing Essays of Synthesis

Introduction. You might open with the question in your planning notes. You can then present facts in the body of your essay, "adding them up" to arrive at your thesis at the end. A second option is to start with your thesis and present supporting reasons in the body of your essay.

Body and conclusion. Be careful not to assume that your viewpoint is the only valid one. Specify the evidence on which you have based your conclusion, opinion, or evaluation. You might devote a paragraph to each reason, stating the reason as a

The following are examples of assignments for essays of synthesis:

• Was the march in Selma, Alabama, the turning point of the civil rights movement of the 1960s? Support your answer.

• In your opinion, should there be a national healthcare system accessible to all people regardless of financial status? Support your answer.

• Was Britain's partition of Palestine after World War II an effective method of dealing with the problems in that area? Support your answer.

generalization, then providing specifics from your notes to back it up. In an evaluation, carefully explain your criteria.

Close your essay by summing up your thinking. If you have not yet presented your thesis, do so in your final paragraph.

Revision Checklist

- Have I stated my thesis, either at the beginning or at the end of my essay?

- Have I included enough specifics to support each generalization that I make? Where might I add more facts, data, or statistics?

- Have I explained my thinking clearly, taking into account other viewpoints that may also be valid?

Book Reports and Reviews

At times you may be asked to write reviews or reports about history books, biographies, or other works of historical interest.

Planning a Book Report or Review

Take brief notes as you read, view, or listen to the material you will respond to. You might note your favorite parts, parts that puzzle you, and (if applicable) parts that bring out strong responses in other viewers or listeners. Afterwards, ask yourself questions to help you analyze and evaluate the material:

- Whose point of view does the material present? Which parts show the point of view?

- What might its purpose be? Which parts show the purpose? What is the author's, artist's, or composer's thesis?

- In the light of its purpose, what are its most—and least—effective aspects?

- What might readers, viewers, or listeners learn from it?

Writing Tip

Simply stating your personal feelings about a book is not enough. You need to support your statements with explanations and references to the work.

Review your notes, and decide on a thesis that you would like to present in your response. Write your thesis as a single sentence on which your report or review will elaborate. List the main points with which you will develop or support your thesis.

Writing a Book Report or Review

Introduction. In your first paragraph, identify the material that you will consider. Name the author, composer, or artist. To orient your reader, provide a summary or brief description of the work. You might also state your thesis in your opening paragraph.

Body. Devote at least a paragraph to each main point. Support each point with details from your prewriting notes—including your own responses—and with examples from the material itself.

Conclusion. If you haven't stated your thesis in the first paragraph, do so in the conclusion. Sum up your judgment of the material's effectiveness and appeal.

Interviews

One excellent way to grasp the nature of primary sources is to create some yourself. When you write interviews, oral histories, and historical narratives, you broaden your own scope, acquiring insight into other time periods and viewpoints.

An interview is a gold mine. It yields nuggets of invaluable insight into the subject's personal experiences and ideas. For some social studies assignments, you might interview living people. For others, you might write imagined interviews with historical figures.

Planning an Interview

The following guidelines will help you plan an interview:

Make an appointment with your subject if you are conducting a real interview (rather than writing an imagined interview). Ask his or her permission to take notes or photos or to make an audiotape or videotape. Practice with your equipment in advance.

> "An interview . . . yields nuggets of invaluable insight into the subject's personal experiences and ideas."

Learn about your subject's life and area of expertise. If you are interviewing an activist or a government official about an issue, for example, learn enough about the issue to ask intelligent questions.

Establish a focus for your questions. In what aspect of your subject's life are you most interested? List questions that focus on it. Avoid questions with yes-or-no answers. Instead, start questions with "Tell me about . . ." or "How did you . . ." or "How do you feel about . . ." Consider sending your questions to your subject ahead of time to let him or her think about them.

Conducting an Interview

Bear the following guidelines in mind when you are conducting your interview:

Set a suitable tone. Arrive on time. If your subject hasn't seen your questions, explain your focus. Then begin with a friendly, open-ended question that will help you and your subject relax.

Sit back and listen. Let your subject do most of the talking, but be responsive so that he or she will be encouraged to go on. If the two of you fall into a spontaneous conversation, feel free to follow it. You can always come back to your list of questions.

Wrap it up. If your interview is to end at a certain time, keep an eye on the clock. Thank your subject, and leave promptly.

Writing an Interview

Introduction. In a brief opening, introduce your subject and provide background information for your readers. Mention the setting—the date and place—of the interview.

Body. If your interview is short, transcribe it in its entirety from your notes or audiotape or videotape, editing out only *uh*'s and *um*'s. You can use a question-and-answer format:

Q: How did you first become interested in politics?
A: I don't think I ever *wasn't* interested. . . .

If your interview is longer, start by transcribing only the parts that seem most important. Then, add other parts that are relevant to your focus. Take care that your omissions don't change the basic thrust of your subject's statements. Avoid selecting "sound bites" that support your own point of view but misrepresent the views of the interviewee. For continuity, you might write "bridges" in which you summarize material you have eliminated. Enclose bridges in parentheses so that your words can't be mistaken for your subject's.

Conclusion. A final thought-provoking quotation from your subject can be an effective conclusion. You might also reflect on your overall impression of the interviewee.

Check your interview for accuracy. If possible, submit your draft to your subject for final approval.

Oral Histories

For an oral history, you interview an eyewitness to a historical event, an era, or a specific way of life. You then present your findings as a narrative—a story—told in the eyewitness's own words. The interviewer usually has a less prominent role in an oral history than in an interview.

Planning and Recording an Oral History

Follow the general interview guidelines on pages 20–21. Your goal is to get your subject to recall a specific event, era, or way of life. As he or she warms to the topic, ask questions to elicit details and explanations.

Writing an Oral History

Introduction. Write a brief opening that introduces your subject and identifies his or her background.

Body. If your subject speaks a dialect, don't "correct" it when you transcribe; dialects and speech mannerisms are part of history. Organize your oral history as a continuous narrative. You might present your subject's memories in chronological order, or you might present them in the order in which your subject recalled them during the interview, following his or her train of thought. Include your questions only if they are needed for clarity.

Writing Tip

When preparing questions for your interviewee, you may find it helpful to focus on specific subject areas, such as early life, school days, social life, work life, home life, and the technological changes the person has witnessed.

Conclusion. Your subject's closing words can be an effective conclusion, as can a brief description of his or her actions at the end of the interview. Include the date and place of the interview.

Historical Narratives

A historical narrative is an account focusing on a particular historical event or issue. It may involve firsthand reporting, as in an account of a political rally in which you participated, or it may involve research and imagination, as in an account of a day in the life of a young person in ancient Rome. Even a narrative that has an imaginative component, however, must also contain factual elements.

One format used for historical narratives is the **monologue**— a speech in which a person reveals thoughts and feelings about an event or issue.

Planning a Historical Narrative or Monologue

Think about the goal of your narrative or monologue. If your work will have an imaginative component—if, for example, it is a monologue by a historical figure—ask yourself whether your primary goal is to convey historical information, to "get inside" a character, or a combination of the two. Because a strong narrative often includes sensory details, you might find it helpful to fill out an observation chart for the events on which your narrative will center. List details relating to all five senses.

OBSERVATION CHART

SENSES	Sight	Hearing	Smell	Taste	Touch
OBSERVATIONS					

" To pull your

readers in, try

starting with

dramatic action. "

Writing a Historical Narrative or Monologue

Introduction. To pull your readers in, try starting with dramatic action—you might, for example, describe a sign-waving demonstrator at a political rally. Include details of time and place to set the scene. You could write from the first-person point of view, using *I, me,* and other first-person pronouns.

Body. Write about events in chronological order. Include transitions that clarify chronological relationships (such as *at first, later, meanwhile,* and *finally*) to keep your readers oriented. Use sensory details from your observation chart to bring events to life, and add your own feelings and thoughts where appropriate. In a monologue, use language suited to the speaker and to his or her circumstances, avoiding, for example, anachronistic words and phrases.

Conclusion. Create a sense of completion with a final comment on the significance of the events or issues presented in the narrative.

Writing Reports

When you write social studies reports, you draw on your research skills and critical-thinking skills as well as your writing skills. This section of *Writing for Social Studies* can help you with the varied tasks that short report writing involves. These tasks are also an essential part of writing longer research papers.

Primary and Secondary Sources

Source materials for social studies research can range from arrowheads to encyclopedia articles. **Primary sources** are firsthand historical materials. **Secondary sources** are books, articles, lectures, and other works that interpret primary sources.

Finding Primary Sources

The field notes of an archaeologist excavating a Viking village are primary sources, as are the artifacts he or she unearths. Letters, wills, tombstone inscriptions, parish registers, newspaper articles, television news reports, government documents, census reports, speeches, court records, portraits, photos, journals, and autobiographies can all be primary sources. These materials, which may offer eyewitness accounts, can give you invaluable insights into historical events. To find primary sources, you might explore any of the following:

- **Museums' and libraries' special collections** often include artifacts, private letters, and original manuscripts. You might examine these in person or via the Internet.

- **Your local historical society** keeps photos, documents, and other materials pertaining to your community.

"Source materials for social studies research can range from arrowheads to encyclopedia articles."

- **Presidential records and other government documents,** available in such reference sources as *Public Papers of the Presidents of the United States* and *Documents of American History,* include materials related to historical and political events. For personal papers of U.S. presidents, you might contact individual presidential libraries or their Web sites.

- **Interviews with eyewitnesses** may be available in your local library on videotape or in back issues of magazines and newspapers. For some topics, you can conduct your own interviews; see "Interviews and Oral Histories," pages 20–23.

- **Statistics and survey results** are available in reference sources such as *Statistical Abstract of the United States,* published each year since 1878, and *World Facts and Figures.* For some topics, you can conduct your own surveys.

- **Period news articles, advertisements, and editorials** can be found in back issues of newspapers, available on microforms in your local library. Back issues of the *New York Times* date to 1851; of the *Chicago Tribune,* to 1847. You can also search the Internet to find newspapers' Web sites devoted to specific historical periods, such as the *Seattle Times* site devoted to World War II.

- **Notes and bibliographies in secondary sources,** such as the chapter notes and references in a nonfiction book, often refer to primary sources and give their locations.

Using Primary Sources

When you work with a primary source, consider questions such as the following:

- **What is the date of the source?** Was it created at or shortly after the time of the event you are investigating, or was it created years later? How might it have been influenced by the values and issues of its time?

- **Who was the author, speaker, or creator of the source?** Was the person an observer of or a participant in the event you are investigating? Does he or she have a reputation for bias? Was he or she an official? If so, does the person give an official stance or "off the record" remarks? If the source is a work of art, music, or literature, was its creator subject to constraints or free to work as he or she pleased?

- **For what audience was the source intended?** A speech for a private audience may differ from a speech for the international media. The views of places, people, and events in a personal letter may differ from those in government records.

- **For what purpose was the source created?** Was it a campaign speech, a piece of propaganda, or a declaration designed to send signals to other nations? If the source is an artifact, was it for everyday use or for a special occasion? If the source is a work of art or literature, was its creator trying to promote a cause?

- **Does the source show bias?** Look for the standard techniques of influencing opinion, such as loaded language, overgeneralization, manipulation of statistics, and circular reasoning. Did the author present opinions as if they were fact? Can the information in the source be verified?

Finding Primary and Secondary Sources

The sources listed in the tables on the following two pages are available in many libraries' reference sections and are useful starting points for social studies research.

American History

Dictionary of American Biography. 20 vols. New York: Scribner's, 1928–37. With 10 supplements to date.

Dictionary of American History. Rev. ed. 8 vols. New York: Scribner's, 1978. Supplement published in 1996.

Documents of American History. Ed. Henry Steele Commager and Milton Cantor. 10th ed. 2 vols. Englewood Cliffs: Prentice-Hall, 1988.

Encyclopedia of Multiculturalism. Ed. Susan Auerbach. 6 vols. New York: Cavendish, 1994.

Encyclopedia of American Scandal. By George Kohn. New York: Facts on File, 1988.

Famous First Facts. By Joseph Nathan Kane. 4th ed. New York: Wilson, 1981.

Historical Atlas of the United States. Rev. ed. Washington: National Geographic Society, 1993.

Historical Statistics of the United States: Colonial Times to 1970. Washington: GPO, 1975.

Official Congressional Directory. Washington: GPO. Published annually, 1887– .

Selected List of U.S. Government Publications. Washington: GPO.

Statistical Abstract of the United States. Washington: GPO. Published yearly, 1878– .

Statistical Record of Asian Americans. Detroit: Gale, 1993.

Statistical Record of Black America. 4th ed. Detroit: Gale, 1997.

Statistical Record of Hispanic Americans. 2nd ed. Detroit: Gale, 1995.

Statistical Record of Native North Americans. Detroit: Gale, 1993.

The United States Government Manual. Washington: GPO. Published annually, 1935– .

Who's Who in America. Chicago: Marquis. Published yearly, 1899– .

World History

Africa Today. 2nd ed. London: Africa, 1991.

Atlas of World History. Chicago: Rand, 1995.

Current Biography. New York: Wilson. Published monthly, 1940– .

Dictionary of the Middle Ages. 13 vols. New York: Scribner's, 1982.

Encyclopedia of Asian History. 4 vols. New York: Scribner's, 1988.

The Encyclopedia of Judaism. New York: Macmillan, 1989.

An Encyclopedia of World History. 5th ed. Boston: Houghton, 1980.

Historical Dictionary of Vietnam. By William J. Duiker. Metuchen : Scarecrow, 1989.

Kodansha Encyclopedia of Japan. 9 vols. New York: Kodansha, 1983.

The Oxford Encyclopedia of the Modern Islamic World. New York: Oxford UP, 1995.

Past Worlds: The Times Atlas of Archaeology. New York: Crescent, 1995.

Webster's New Biographical Dictionary. Springfield: Merriam, 1988.

Who Was When?: A Dictionary of Contemporaries. 3rd ed. New York: Wilson, 1976.

Who's Who. London: Black. Published yearly, 1849– .

World Facts and Figures. By Victor Showers. 3rd ed. New York: Wiley, 1989.

Yearbook of the United Nations. New York: UN Office of Public Information. Published yearly, 1947– .

The Internet as a Source

By using a search engine to access sources on the World Wide Web or elsewhere on the Internet, you can locate specialized information—including both primary and secondary sources—in university libraries, museums, and research institutions around the world. This information may include photos, sound recordings, and videos as well as written texts.

The Internet can provide you with a wealth of sources, but be sure to carefully evaluate all material you find on-line. Many sites on the World Wide Web have not been edited in the way that most books have. For this reason, many Web sites—in particular those maintained by individuals—contain inaccurate or biased information. Ask yourself the following questions:

- Is this material presented by a nationally or internationally respected source, such as an accredited university or other responsible institution? (If you're not sure, a research librarian can help you find out.)

- Do I detect bias in this material? (For more on detecting bias, see page 64.)

- How might I verify the accuracy of this material?

Short Reports

Every time you read a newspaper article, a magazine article, or a nonfiction book, you are reading a report. The author has gathered information from various sources, analyzed and interpreted it, and used a particular format to present his or her findings. Pages 35–143 of this booklet lead you through the process of writing a research report; this section is a quick guide to the writing of short reports. The tasks discussed here, however, will also form the basis of your work on research reports.

When you write a short report, you are like a journalist writing a magazine article. You choose a topic, analyze information from two or more sources, and present the information in a way that makes it significant, clear, and memorable.

Planning a Short Report

The topic of a short report must be narrow enough for you to cover it thoroughly in just a few pages. You might start by reading an encyclopedia article on your topic. (Remember to read the article only for ideas. Do not just copy the text.) Notice the headings under which the topic is broken down; one of the headings may suggest a narrower topic. In narrowing your topic, you might also consider the purpose of your writing, as shown in the following table.

Research Tip

Some encyclopedias are available on-line or on CD-ROM. Check what resources are available at your school or local library.

Broad Topic: Propaganda in World War II

PURPOSE	NARROWER TOPIC
• To analyze cause and effect • To compare and contrast • To clarify	• Reasons why Tokyo Rose was used by the Japanese • Posters: Allied versus Axis • Types of propaganda used at home by the Allies

Once you have narrowed your topic, write a **statement of controlling purpose,** telling briefly what your report will cover. This statement can keep you on track as you research your topic. Later, it will become the basis of your thesis statement.

Start your research by listing questions that you hope to answer in your report. Then find primary and secondary sources of information. Check your library's catalog and reference section, the *Readers' Guide to Periodical Literature,* the *New York Times Index,* and the World Wide Web. Other sources include local historical sites, museums, personal interviews, and surveys.

For each source you use, make a bibliography card (see pages 64–66 for instructions and models). Bibliography cards save you time in note taking and in creating your Works Cited list. To save more time, don't read your sources all the way through; focus only on sections pertaining to your topic.

Take careful notes, identifying the source of each. (See pages 70–71 for more on note taking.) Print out material from the Internet, jotting down the date and the source's address on the printout. For other material, use the techniques of summary, paraphrase, and quotation explained on page 70.

Organizing a Short Report

When you finish your research, review your notes. Taking into account what you have discovered, rewrite your statement of controlling purpose as a **thesis statement**—a sentence or two that clearly states the main idea your report will present. Then list the major points you will make in developing your thesis, and group your notes according to the points they support.

Plan the order in which you will present your points—an order in which each idea flows logically to the next. To make writing easier, jot down an informal outline in which you list your points and supporting information in the order you have chosen. If you prefer working from a more formal outline, see the guidelines for constructing topic outlines and sentence outlines on pages 76–78.

Writing a Short Report

Introduction. To catch your readers' attention, you might open with a surprising statistic, a quotation, or a memorable image related to your thesis. Include your thesis statement near the opening of your report.

Body. As you write, stay flexible. You are presenting not only information but also your own analysis and interpretations. If a new idea pops up as you write, feel free to try it out. If you can't find a way to integrate it into your report, you can revise your organization plan, or even your thesis, or you can go back to your original outline. Don't forget to include graphic devices if they will make your report more interesting or understandable.

Write at least one paragraph for each point, using transition words to show how your ideas are related. Support each of your points with information from your research, and document the sources of all your information. For guidelines on documenting sources, see pages 95–102.

Conclusion. You might close by summarizing your research or by restating your thesis in different words. Alternatively, you might create a sense of completion by referring again to the statistic, quotation, or image with which you started, briefly noting how your information illuminates its significance. Add a Works Cited list at the end of your report (see pages 100–102).

Multimedia Reports

Instead of writing a traditional report, you may want to present your information in a multimedia report. A multimedia report combines text, sound, and visuals. Your audience uses a computer to read, hear, and see your material, clicking on links to move from

> " As you write, stay flexible. "

part to part of the report. The links can be highlighted words, navigational buttons, or graphic images.

For a multimedia report, you need computer programs to create and edit the text, the graphics, and the sound and video files you will use. You also need a multimedia authoring program that allows you to combine these elements and to link your screens. Ask your school's technology adviser which of the following elements are available to you:

Sound. Including sound in your presentation can help your audience understand the information in your written text. For example, you might include a recording of a famous speech or one that clarifies the pronunciation of a foreign word.

Photos and videos. Photographs and live-action video clips can make your subject come alive. For example, you might include photographs of artifacts or images of original documents. If you have videotaped an interview, you might include clips of the interview in your presentation.

Animation. Many graphics programs allow you to add animation to your presentation. You might use animation to illustrate the steps in a process or trace a route on a map.

Planning a Multimedia Report

One starting point for a multimedia report is something that you have written; in such a case, your aim in creating the multimedia report is to enhance the written material by adding sound and visuals. At other times, you may plan to present your material in a multimedia report from the outset.

When you have an idea of the material you wish to cover, you must plan how you want your audience to move through the report. There are two basic ways of organizing a multimedia report:

- in step-by-step fashion, with only one path for the audience to follow from screen to screen
- in branching fashion, so that the audience can, to a certain extent, choose what they will see and hear and the order in which they will experience it

> "Photographs and live-action video clips can make your subject come alive."

33

If you choose the second way—an interactive presentation—you need to map out your report in a flow chart or navigation map, as shown below. This will help you plan the links that will allow your audience to choose paths through the parts of your report.

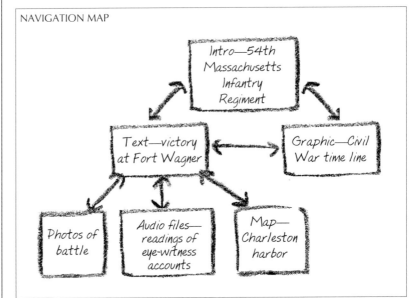

NAVIGATION MAP

Intro—54th Massachusetts Infantry Regiment

Text—victory at Fort Wagner

Graphic—Civil War time line

Photos of battle

Audio files—readings of eye-witness accounts

Map—Charleston harbor

Research Tip

CD-ROMs and the Internet are useful sources of material for a multimedia report. On CD-ROMs you can find video clips whose subjects range from historic events to street scenes, as well as audio recordings of live performances and famous speeches. From the Internet you can download photos, sound files, and video files. Keep notes of your sources.

Creating a Multimedia Report

After you decide on the content of a screen, you will find it helpful to sketch the design of the screen. Remember to include in your sketch the links that will lead to other parts of the presentation. Use your navigation map as a guide to help you decide what links you need to add in each screen.

Make sure that the first screen gives the title of the report and identifies its focus. In this respect, it serves the same purpose as the opening paragraph of a written report. The first screen should also explain how your audience can move through the report. You might also add to your report a screen or set of notes listing the sources of your information.

Writing Research Papers

The rest of this booklet is a comprehensive guide to the process of writing a research paper. It leads you through all of the stages, from finding a topic to preparing the final manuscript.

Understanding the Research Paper

Have you ever written a report in which you drew upon several different sources? If so, you have already produced something like a research paper. A research paper is a written report that presents the results of a purposeful, focused, in-depth study of a specific topic. Its writer chooses a topic, gathers information about the topic from several different sources, and then presents that information in an organized way.

Writing a research paper will most likely be the most time-consuming and challenging task that you have ever undertaken as a student. Don't let the size of the task scare you, though. You will find researching and writing your paper quite easy if you take it one step at a time, following the guidelines in this book.

Research and the Writing Process

Some types of writing, like taking notes in class or jotting down a grocery list, are done all at once. However, most types of writing are done over a longer period of time. In other words, writing is a process, and it can be roughly divided into stages—prewriting, drafting, revising, proofreading, and publishing. This book will take you through the following activities in the process of writing a research paper.

> "Don't let the size of the task scare you. . . . You will find researching and writing your paper quite easy if you take it one step at a time, following the guidelines in this book."

The Research Process

- Choosing your subject
- Doing preliminary research
- Limiting your subject to a specific topic

<blockquote>
"Writing is a process, and it can be roughly divided into stages—prewriting, drafting, revising, proofreading, and publishing."
</blockquote>

The Research Process (cont.)

- Finding an angle and writing a statement of controlling purpose
- Preparing a list of possible sources (a working bibliography)
- Taking notes and developing a rough, or working, outline
- Organizing your notes and making a final outline
- Writing your first draft
- Revising your draft
- Writing the final draft with a complete list of works cited

As you work through the next few chapters, you will come to understand more clearly what constitutes a successful research paper. For now, read the sample research paper on the following pages. Then answer the questions at the end of the paper.

J. Robert Oppenheimer and General Leslie Groves survey a nuclear test site. Not yet fully aware of the effects of nuclear fallout, they wear baggies to protect their feet.

Sarah Ryan

Mr. Dalicandro

American History

13 May 1998

The Road to Hiroshima

In August 1945, after three and a half brutal years of participation in World War II, the United States dropped atomic bombs on Hiroshima and Nagasaki, Japan. The bombs ended the war, but the cost was higher than anyone had foreseen. Hundreds of thousands of civilians were killed by the blasts and the effects of radiation ("World War II"). Almost at once, a deadly nuclear-arms race began.

Why did the United States take such a drastic step? President Harry S. Truman later accepted full responsibility. "The final decision of where and when to use the bomb," he maintained in his memoirs, "was up to me" (419). Yet the bombing of Japan was anything but a one-person decision. The story behind the decision to use the bomb is far more complex than Truman's simple statement suggests. A number of people were involved in the decision to use the atomic bomb, and their deliberations involved a number of ethical, political, and military issues.

An understanding of why the bomb was dropped requires an understanding of why it was built. The groundwork was laid before anyone knew there would be a World War II. In one sense the bomb was a natural outcome of landmark discoveries in physics. Scientists of the 1920s and 1930s had learned that the cores of atoms are not solid, as had been thought previously. Atomic nuclei are really clumps of smaller particles—protons and neutrons. Scientists soon realized that the nuclei could be broken apart and that the splitting of the nuclei, a process called fission, would

Sample Paper

The first paragraph presents basic facts to create a context for the thesis statement.

This citation refers to an unsigned and unpaginated on-line source.

If the author of a source is named in the text of the paper, the citation need include only the number(s) of the page(s) on which the information can be found.

Thesis statement

This sentence suggests that the paper will, in general, be organized chronologically.

In this paragraph, the writer uses cause-and-effect order as well as chronological order to explain the scientific discoveries that made the atomic bomb possible.

release energy. Since the bonds joining the particles are powerful, the energy released when the bonds are broken would also be powerful.

In the late 1930s, fascinated physicists throughout the world were exploring nuclear fission. Meanwhile, the political scene was shifting in ways that would give their research new significance. The troops of Nazi Germany, led by Adolf Hitler, were on the march in Europe. In September 1939, Britain and France declared war on Germany, and World War II began.

By that time, research suggested that nuclear fission could create an immensely powerful bomb. Physicists such as Leo Szilard and Edward Teller of Hungary and Rudolf Peierls and Albert Einstein of Germany, who had fled the Nazis, knew that Nazi physicists would also see the potential for fission bombs. They alerted the governments of the United States and Britain (Clark 109). A fission bomb could be made from uranium, the physicists explained, and Nazi researchers had access to uranium. In a letter to President Franklin D. Roosevelt, Einstein warned that ". . . extremely powerful bombs of a new type may thus be constructed. A single bomb of this type, carried by boat and exploded in a port, might very well destroy the whole port together with some of the surrounding territory." (1)

Allied leaders listened. At the time, bombs were made with conventional explosives, and the most powerful had a force equivalent to that of three tons of TNT. Now physicists were describing a bomb potentially more powerful than a hundred tons of TNT (Clark 95). If such a bomb could be built, Allied leaders wanted to build it before the Nazis did. By 1940, the United States and Britain had

This paragraph provides background information that helps the reader to get his or her bearings.

This is the standard form for parenthetical documentation. The author's last name is followed by the number(s) of the page(s) on which the information can be found.

The writer quotes from a primary source to elaborate on her point.

authorized extra funds for fission research, to be applied
to the development of an atomic bomb (Larsen 42).

Scientists already conducting fission research were
asked to participate in the US and British bomb projects.
Some accepted for practical reasons; others, for scientific
reasons. As Teller explained in a later interview, "I
believe that . . . scientists have the responsibility of
developing tools for mankind" (76). In addition, many of
the scientists were refugees from Nazi and Fascist
brutality. They feared what a fission bomb in enemy hands
could do, and they assumed that in Allied hands such a bomb
would be the quickest means of achieving peace. They
expected that world leaders would understand the bomb's
potential for global destruction, so that the bomb's mere
existence would end the war.

As a result, well before the United States entered
World War II in December 1941, American atomic-bomb
research was underway. In 1942, Szilard and Enrico Fermi
(who had recently fled Fascist Italy), along with colleagues
at the University of Chicago, created a "nuclear pile" of
uranium and graphite in which they could start, stop, and
control the kind of fission chain reaction needed for a
working atomic bomb (Phillips 164-65). Their success,
together with the fear that German researchers might
complete an atomic bomb first, moved the bomb project
quickly from research into development.

The production of bomb-quality uranium was expensive
and required special factories, but Roosevelt was willing
to fund it. By early 1943 the three parts of a top-secret
bomb development project, code-named Manhattan, were in
place: (1) the continuation of research at the University
of Chicago, (2) the production of uranium at Oak Ridge,

In this paragraph cause-and-effect organization is used to to explore the motives of the groups involved in A-bomb research.

The points of ellipsis (. . .) show that some words have been omitted in the quotation.

When information is taken from consecutive pages of a source, cite the pages on which the information begins and ends, joined by a hyphen.

Sample Paper

Tennessee, and Hanford, Washington, and (3) the construction of the bomb itself at Los Alamos, New Mexico. British experts were soon invited to join the US team (Clark 154).

The organization of the Manhattan Project was to become a key factor in determining the final use of the bomb. From the beginning of the development phase, the project was in military hands as well as in the hands of civilian scientists. The scientists tended to call for restraint and caution regarding the bomb. The military, however, took it for granted that the bomb would be a significant weapon of war. Conflicts between the two groups' viewpoints would intensify as the bomb was built.

The US Army Corps of Engineers took over the Manhattan Project in the fall of 1942. Supervision was shared by the US Army general Leslie Groves and the American physicist J. Robert Oppenheimer, both working in Los Alamos. They reported to a small Military Policy Committee (MPC) headed by the former MIT dean Vannevar Bush, who was now the director of the Office of Scientific Research and Development. James Conant and Henry Stimson also sat in on MPC meetings (Beyer 37-38). Conant, a former president of Harvard University, chaired the National Defense Research Council, and Stimson, a graduate of both Yale and Harvard, was Roosevelt's highly respected secretary of war. Stimson had been a diplomat and student of world history and culture for over thirty years ("Stimson"). Bush, Conant, and Stimson would participate in the 1945 discussion of the political, ethical, and humanitarian aspects of dropping the A-bomb on Japan. In 1942, however, as the Manhattan Project gained momentum, the only plan was to use the bomb somehow to stop the relentless advance of Hitler.

This paragraph begins the second section of the paper, which traces the steps in the development of the bomb.

In general, each major section of a research paper should begin with a transitional sentence or paragraph presenting the section's main idea.

To document unsigned, unpaginated material from a CD-ROM, give a shortened form of the material's title.

Sample
Paper

The MPC regularly briefed Roosevelt, and Roosevelt
shared his information with British prime minister Winston
Churchill. In August 1943, these two quietly signed the
Quebec Agreement, a pledge that they would collaborate on
atomic weapons and that neither would use such weapons or
reveal information about them without the consent of the
other (Beyer 589). The agreement would affect at least one
decision about the use of the bomb.

As the atomic bomb approached completion, few people
clearly foresaw the consequences that it would have in the
postwar world. The Danish physicist and Nobel laureate
Niels Bohr was one who did. Early in 1944 he contacted both
Roosevelt and Churchill and pointed out that other
countries would soon create their own atomic bombs. He
urged that the nuclear threat be discussed openly so that
an international set of checks and balances, which he saw
as the hope of the future, could be devised (Beyer 59-60).
Roosevelt at first agreed with Bohr, but Churchill's
response was very different. Unwilling to weaken the impact
of the new weapon by releasing information about it, he
suggested that Bohr be watched as a possible traitor.
Although Bohr, a leading figure in the Danish resistance
movement, was quickly cleared, Churchill never changed his
intention to use the atomic bomb in the same way that
conventional bombs were being used—that is, to drop it on
one or more enemy cities. Roosevelt understood that
Churchill's view was shortsighted and that this bomb was
unlike any weapon previously known. Because of the Quebec
Agreement, however, he supported Churchill over the Danish
scientist (Rhodes 529-31).

By the spring of 1945, Oppenheimer and his team in Los
Alamos had constructed two atomic bombs, with a third near

This paragraph begins
the third section of the
paper, which explores
the controversies that
erupted over the
possible consequences
of using the bomb.

completion (Clark 155). Simultaneously, the course of the war was shifting. The Allied commander in chief in Europe, Dwight D. Eisenhower, had led a successful invasion of the continent, and on May 7 Germany surrendered. The bomb was no longer needed to stop Hitler. In the Pacific, however, Japan was proving a fiercer adversary than had been anticipated. Determined Japanese forces regularly fought to the death rather than surrender. US troops were advancing toward Japan, but the cost in human lives was unprecedented. With Germany out of the picture, General Groves and other US military leaders turned to the bomb as a means of stopping the bloodshed in the Pacific.

A further complication had arisen in April 1945, with the sudden death of President Roosevelt, who had not told Vice-President Truman about the Manhattan Project. During Truman's first week as president, he learned of the bomb from Stimson and from the presidential adviser James Byrnes. Stimson focused on the bomb's potential for global destruction and the need for careful planning and foresight. Byrnes, on the other hand, stressed that the bomb could allow the United States to dictate its own terms at the end of the war (Rhodes 617-18).

Only weeks before Roosevelt's death, Szilard, of the Manhattan Project's Chicago group, had begun an effort to convince the president not to use the bomb. Both Szilard's and Bohr's concerns were for the future. They foresaw an international nuclear-arms race and wanted to create a panel of scientists to aid the president in developing arms controls. Unfortunately, Szilard had just found a way to reach Roosevelt when a radio broadcast announced the president's death. In May 1945, Szilard finally managed to contact Truman. Truman referred him to Byrnes, who doubted the scientist's predictions and considered his suggestions insulting. Szilard next talked to Oppenheimer in Los Alamos but found him committed to dropping the bomb (Lanouette 259-67). At this point, Szilard stopped trying to bring about changes in the policy—temporarily.

By the time Truman learned the details of the Manhattan Project, General Groves had already formed a military Target Committee to choose Japanese cities as targets for atomic bombing (Lanouette 264). Groves had no doubts about using the bomb on Japanese cities. As project supervisor he felt responsible for the expenditure of the two billion dollars it had cost to build the bomb. He would not have found it easy to justify such a huge expenditure— over one-fifth the cost of running the entire federal government for a year—on a single weapon that was never used (Phillips 10).

Truman and Churchill had other reasons for wanting to use the bomb. The USSR, led by Joseph Stalin, was alarming the Allies by aggressively moving into countries formerly occupied by Germany. It appeared that in order to defeat Japan, Truman and Churchill would need Stalin's help (Larsen 81, 91). Under these circumstances they were in no position to demand that he end his aggression in Europe. An atomic bomb, however, would make his help unnecessary and might even intimidate him.

At Stimson's suggestion Truman convened an advisory group, the Interim Committee, to evaluate possible ways of employing the bomb. Its members included the familiar trio of Stimson, Bush, and Conant, as well as Byrnes (now secretary of state), Undersecretary of the Navy Ralph Bard, and the Manhattan Project scientists Oppenheimer and Fermi. General Groves often sat in on Interim Committee meetings

This documentation refers to source material that the writer has summarized.

When information is taken from nonconsecutive pages of a source, cite all relevant pages, separating the numbers with commas.

Sample Paper

43

as an adviser, and Oppenheimer sat in on Target Committee meetings (Rhodes 628-29). In this way, like the Manhattan Project, both of the groups devising policies for the use of the world's first atomic weapons received both military and civilian input.

In the next month, the Interim Committee debated ethical and practical aspects of the use of the bomb, as Byrnes recalled:

> Then there was a question of giving the Japanese fair
> warning about the time and place of the explosion,
> but we rejected it because we feared the American
> prisoners of war would be brought into the designated
> area. We were told by experts, too, that . . . they
> could not guarantee that . . . [the] bomb would
> explode when dropped. . . .
>
>   If we gave the Japanese advance notice of the time
> and place we would drop the bomb, and then the bomb
> failed to explode, . . . Japanese militarists . . .
> would say that our failure was proof that we were
> merely bluffing about possessing the bomb. (65)

As scientists described the power of the bomb and the effects of the radiation it would release, the committee members sat stunned. Stimson felt that if the bomb were used at all, it would have to be used in a "precision-style" bombing of a military target, such as a weapons plant, to spare human lives (Rhodes 650). Byrnes considered with horror an idea he had previously considered impossible—that the USSR might soon develop an atomic bomb to use against the United States. To him, quickly establishing dominance seemed the only defense, since ". . . so far as the Soviet Union is concerned, they respect only power" (67).

For a quotation of more than four lines, begin a new line and indent the quotation ten spaces from the left margin. Place the parenthetical documentation at the end of the quotation.

The brackets enclose a slight modification made to the source in order to avoid an ungrammatical construction.

When quoting more than one paragraph, indicate each paragraph break by indenting the line an additional three spaces.

When Stimson consulted military leaders about precision bombing, he was told that in Japan weapons manufacturing was a cottage industry, carried out in private homes, so that precision bombing of weapons factories was not feasible (Rhodes 649-50). Meanwhile, Byrnes pressed the Interim Committee to come to a decision. He urged that the bomb be used without warning, the sooner the better. Thousands of American lives were being lost daily. Oppenheimer had speculated that the bomb might kill around 20,000 people (Larsen 112). Byrnes maintained that the only alternative to using the bomb was a US invasion of Japan, an operation in which, according to military leaders, a million American soldiers might be killed or wounded (Beyer 62).

In later years, Szilard was to call options of nuclear attack and invasion "the fake alternatives" (Interview 70). Basically, he was right: invasion was not the only alternative to using the bomb, nor was it the best one available. Japan's air force and navy were crippled, and an Allied blockade was having devastating effects. Furthermore, in March 1945, the US general Curtis LeMay had devised a means of firebombing that, he felt, could defeat Japan without the need for invasion (Rhodes 600; Phillips 266). Stimson, opposed to the bombing of civilians, had ordered him to hold off, but LeMay firebombed Tokyo on May 25, reducing much of the Japanese capital to rubble. American newspapers announced the attack in triumphant headlines. In spite of this news and its implications, the Interim Committee's final recommendation, issued on June 1, 1945, was to drop the atomic bomb on one or more Japanese cities with no warning (Beyer 64).

Shortly before the Interim Committee issued its report, Groves's Target Committee had finalized a choice of

The paper includes material from more than one source attributed to Szilard, so the citation identifies the relevant source.

When material from two sources is documented in a citation, the two references should be separated with a semicolon.

45

Japanese cities: Hiroshima, Kokura, Niigata, and Nagasaki. Each housed military installations but had not yet sustained major war damage. The Target Committee wanted the bomb's effects to be clear—to themselves and to the world. Tokyo, already destroyed by firebombing, was off the list. Kyoto, Japan's 1,200-year-old cultural center, and the home of irreplaceable historical treasures, had originally headed the list but had been removed by an outraged Stimson (Rhodes 641).

Truman gave both committees' recommendations careful attention but stated no decision. Opposition to the Interim Committee's report arose almost instantly. Bohr tried to contact Stimson, still hoping to prevent the use of the bomb, at least until a means of arms control was in place (Rhodes 651). Bard withdrew his support of the report and went so far as to resign as undersecretary of the navy. He felt that Japan was already seeking a way to surrender and that a surprise bombing would be inconsistent with the "position of the United States as a great humanitarian nation and the fair play attitude of our people" (qtd. in "Was A-Bomb" 74). On June 11, 1945, a committee of seven Manhattan Project scientists at the University of Chicago issued a memorandum now called the Franck Report. This report outlined the dangers of the atomic bomb and the inevitability of a nuclear-arms race and urged that Japan be given a harmless demonstration of an atomic explosion and that nuclear arms controls be devised (Franck et al.).

At Los Alamos the scientists on the Interim Committee conferred about devising an atomic-blast demonstration. Within a month, however, they concluded that they couldn't quickly prepare an atomic explosion that was certain to work. Preparations were underway to test one of the three

When documenting material from an unsigned periodical article, cite the title of the article and the relevant page number.

46

Sample Paper

existing bombs. The test was planned to coincide with a conference that Truman, Churchill, and Stalin were holding in Potsdam, Germany. On July 16, 1945, in the high desert near Alamogordo, New Mexico, the world's first atomic bomb exploded with an intensity that stunned even Oppenheimer (Larsen 94-95). On the same day, the uranium cores of the remaining atomic bombs were loaded aboard a ship bound for Tinian Island, the Pacific airbase from which US bombers took off for Japan. The other bomb parts had been sent ahead weeks earlier (Rhodes 662, 678). Fliers based on Tinian were already practicing techniques they would use to drop the bomb (Beyer 69-70). No order to bomb Japan had yet been given, but the military expected one and would be ready.

By July 17, Szilard had prepared a petition, signed by 69 other Manhattan Project scientists, that asked Truman not to use the bomb "without seriously considering the moral responsibilities which are involved" ("Petition"). Truman, in Germany at the time, had no chance to see the petition until August (Lanouette 275). However, Groves had seen an earlier version of the petition and had responded much as Churchill had responded to Bohr: he considered charging Szilard with treason. In a July 4 letter to Lord Cherwell, Churchill's science advisor and a former employer of Szilard, Groves asked about Szilard's activities, adding, "Frankly, Dr. Szilard has not, in our opinion, evidenced wholehearted cooperation in the maintenance of security." Cherwell calmed Groves by replying that Szilard "always had rather a bee in his bonnet about the awful implications of these [fission-related] matters" but that "his security was good."

In Potsdam, Truman was elated to learn of the Alamogordo test. He and Churchill could now take a stronger

The writer quotes from primary sources to illustrate the nature of the controversy.

Brackets are used to enclose words that a writer adds to a quotation to make its meaning clear to the reader.

47

stance against Stalin. Through July 26, 1945, the three worked at hammering out the futures of the European countries that had fallen under Axis control. They also formulated the Potsdam Declaration, demanding Japan's immediate "unconditional surrender" and threatening "prompt and utter destruction" if Japan failed to comply (qtd. in Rhodes 692). This was as close as anyone came to warning Japan about the atomic bomb. On July 25, a day before the release of the Potsdam Declaration, Truman had already authorized the use of the bomb in early August if Japan did not capitulate (Clark 210).

Stimson anticipated a problem with the Potsdam Declaration, believing that Japan's leaders would never accept terms that might allow their emperor to be tried, imprisoned, or executed. He therefore advised Truman to clarify the phrase "unconditional surrender" to specify that the emperor's safety and dignity were guaranteed— which, in fact, they were (Rhodes 686, 689). The Allies wanted only to disarm Japan, not to take revenge on the emperor. Truman, however, apparently disregarded Stimson's suggestion. It was never carried out.

The result was as Stimson had foreseen. On July 28 the Japanese, unable to accept the wording of the declaration, issued a refusal to surrender (Rhodes 693). An assistant to the deputy chief of staff of the Japanese army, Sakoh Tanemura, later confirmed that Japan would have surrendered if the Allies had guaranteed "the safety and status of the Emperor" ("Was A-Bomb" 65). And so, spurred on by what may have been simply misinterpretation of language, the United States and Japan passed the point of no return. Within a week, a mushroom cloud would fill the sky over Hiroshima.

When documenting material quoted by an author, rather than written by him or her, add *qtd. in* before the citation.

48

The details of this long story leave several questions unanswered, but they show one thing clearly: the decision to drop the atomic bomb was neither simple nor hasty. Like the bomb itself, the decision was the result of a complex chain of events. Certainly President Truman showed courage in taking sole responsibility for the nuclear horrors that engulfed Hiroshima and Nagasaki. However, the resolution to drop the bomb involved careful consideration of the issues——ethical, political, and military——by numerous people, all no doubt aware that their decision would have an irrevocable effect on the future of humanity.

In the concluding paragraph, the writer restates her thesis in different words. She also sums up the information presented in the paper and adds final reflections.

Works Cited

Beyer, Don E. The Manhattan Project. New York: Watts,
        1991.

Byrnes, James F. Interview. "Was a Bomb" 65-68.

Cherwell, Lord [Frederick Lindemann]. Letter to Leslie
        R. Groves. 12 July 1945. Online. Atomic Bomb:
        Decision. Internet. 3 May 1998. Available
        http://www.peak.org/~danneng/decision/lrg-fal.html.

Clark, Ronald W. The Greatest Power on Earth: The
        International Race for Nuclear Supremacy. New York:
        Harper, 1980.

Einstein, Albert. Letter to Franklin D. Roosevelt. 2 Aug.
        1939. Online. Frontiers: Research Highlights of
        Argonne National Laboratory. Internet. 3 May 1998.
        Available http://www.anl.gov/OPA/frontiers96/
        aetofdr.html.

Franck, James, et. al. Report of the Committee on
        Political and Social Problems, Manhattan Project
        "Metallurgical Laboratory," University of Chicago. 11
        June 1945. Online. Atomic Bomb: Decision. Internet. 3
        May 1998. Available http://www.peak.org/~danneng/
        franck.html.

Groves, Leslie R. Letter to Lord Cherwell. 4 July 1945.
        Online. Atomic Bomb: Decision. Internet. 3 May 1998.
        Available http://www.peak.org/~danneng/decision/
        lrg-fal.html.

Lanouette, William. Genius in the Shadows: A Biography of
        Leo Szilard, the Man behind the Bomb. New York:
        Scribner's, 1992.

Larsen, Rebecca. Oppenheimer and the Atomic Bomb. New
        York: Watts, 1988.

Book

Interview in a
periodical (in this case,
in an article for which
a full reference is given
elsewhere)

Primary source
accessed on Internet
(including, if your
instructor requires it,
the Internet address
where the source can
be found)

Phillips, Cabell. <u>The 1940s: Decade of Triumph and</u>
      <u>Trouble</u>. New York: Macmillan, 1975.

Rhodes, Richard. <u>The Making of the Atomic Bomb</u>. New York:
      Simon, 1986.

"Stimson, Henry." <u>New Grolier Multimedia Encyclopedia</u>.
      1991 ed. CD-ROM. Danbury: Grolier Electronic, 1991.

Szilard, Leo. Interview. "Was A-Bomb" 68-71.

---. "A Petition to the President of the United States."
      17 July 1945. Online. <u>Atomic Bomb: Decision</u>.
      Internet. 3 May 1998. Available
      http://www.peak.org/~danneng/45-07-17.html.

Teller, Edward. Interview. "Was A-Bomb" 75-76.

Truman, Harry S. <u>Year of Decisions</u>. Garden City:
      Doubleday, 1955. Vol. 1 of <u>Memoirs</u>. 2 vols. 1955-56.

"Was A-Bomb on Japan a Mistake?" <u>US News and World Report</u>
      15 Aug. 1960: 62-76.

"World War II." <u>Compton's Online Encyclopedia</u>. Online.
      America Online. 3 May 1998.

CD-ROM

Three hyphens used to
indicate same name as
in preceding entry

Unsigned periodical
article

On-line
information service

Think and Respond

In your learning log, in your writing folder, or in a group discussion, analyze the sample research paper on the previous pages. Respond to these questions about the paper:

1. What information appears in the heading of the paper? at the top of each page?

2. What is the main idea, or thesis, of the paper? Does the writer support her thesis? How?

3. What are the three major parts of the body of the paper? What is the main idea in each part? Does the order of the parts make sense? Why or why not?

4. How does the writer of the paper indicate, within the paper, that she has taken material from a source?

5. Where does the writer's complete list of sources appear, and what is it called?

6. Does the writer use a wide variety of sources? What different kinds of sources does she use?

7. How does the writer introduce her paper?

8. How does the writer conclude her paper?

9. Does the writer use evidence skillfully to support the claims that she makes? Give two examples.

10. What suggestions for improvement might you give this writer?

As president, Harry S. Truman was greatly respected for his decisiveness and willingness to accept responsibility for his decisions ("The Buck Stops Here" read a sign on his desk).

Discovering a Topic for Research

O ne of the most important parts of doing a research paper is choosing a topic. By choosing wisely, you can ensure that your research will go smoothly and that you will enjoy doing it.

Choosing a Subject That You Care About

A **subject** is a broad area of interest, such as African-American history or U.S. politicians. One way to approach the search for a research paper topic is first to choose a general area of interest and then to focus on some part of it. Make sure that you have a real reason for wanting to explore the subject. Often the best subjects for research papers are ones that are related to your own life or to the lives of people you know.

If you are already keeping a "writing ideas" section in your journal or in your writing portfolio, you can refer to that list for possible subjects. If you are not regularly listing your writing ideas, you might consider starting to do so now.

You can begin exploring general subject areas that interest you by completing the following interest inventory.

> " Often the best subjects for research papers are ones that are related to your own life or to the lives of people you know. "

Interest Inventory

Respond in writing to the following questions:

1. What subjects do I enjoy reading about?

2. What topics that I have recently read about in magazines or seen on television would I like to know more about?

" If I could have

a long conversation

with someone from

any place and from

any time in history,

who would that

person be? "

Interest Inventory (cont.)

3. What books have I enjoyed reading in the past?

4. What subjects have captured my attention and interest in my classes?

5. What issues do I feel strongly about?

6. What kind of topic do I want to write about—an event, a person, a government policy, or an idea?

7. What interesting careers or hobbies do my friends, acquaintances, and relatives have? What interesting experiences have they had?

8. If I could have a long conversation with someone from any place and from any time in history, who would that person be?

9. What do I wonder about? What aspects of my world would I like to know the origins or history of?

If your answers to the interest inventory questions don't suggest a general subject area that you would like to learn more about, try the following activities.

Searching for a Subject

1. Spend some time in a library, simply walking up and down the aisles or browsing through the catalog, looking for subjects that appeal to you.

2. Browse through encyclopedias, almanacs, atlases, dictionaries, or recent periodical indexes. Useful indexes include the *Readers' Guide to Periodical Literature* and *Historical Abstracts*.

Searching for a Subject (cont.)

3. If your school or library has any books with lists of ideas for research papers, look through these.

4. Glance at the tables of contents of your textbooks, looking for subjects that you'd like to know more about.

5. If you have access to an electronic encyclopedia, a knowledge database, or a computer index that covers general subjects, start with an interesting search word and see where that leads. If you have access to the Internet, you could try browsing the World Wide Web for topics that interest you.

6. Watch some public television specials about history, or listen to some public radio programs about history. See if any of the subjects of the programs capture your imagination.

7. Look through newsmagazines for subjects related to current events.

8. List some novels that you have read or films that you have seen, and think about possible subjects related to these.

> "Spend some time in a library, simply walking up and down the aisles or browsing through the catalog, looking for subjects that appeal to you."

Limiting Your Subject/Choosing a Topic

Once you have a **general subject** that you are interested in, such as migrant workers or civil rights, the next step is to narrow that subject to a **specific topic** that can be treated in a research paper.

Doing Preliminary Research

If you already know a great deal about your subject, then you can probably think of a specific topic to research in that subject area. However, if you are not already an expert, it is a good idea to do some preliminary research to identify potential topics. Here are a few suggestions for preliminary research.

Research Tip

You may want to start your topic search by choosing a general subject area in one of these categories:

History

Government

Geography

Sociology

Remember that many social studies research papers involve research in other subject areas, such as literature, science, and the arts.

Ideas for Preliminary Research

- Read encyclopedia articles.

- List questions about the subject, and interview someone knowledgeable about it.

- Brainstorm with friends, classmates, or relatives to find out what they know about the subject.

- Check the *Readers' Guide to Periodical Literature* to find general articles on your subject.

- Find a textbook that covers the general field of study to which your subject belongs. Read about your subject in that textbook.

- Go to the place in the library where books on the subject are shelved. Choose books at random and look them over.

Here is how one student conducted her preliminary research.

One Student's Process: Sarah

While completing her interest inventory, Sarah paused at the question about relatives' interesting experiences. Her grandfather had been a GI in World War II, and in 1945 his orders to go to the Pacific theater had been changed after the dropping of atomic bombs on Hiroshima and Nagasaki. The war had soon ended, and her grandfather had returned to the United States. Sarah realized that in addition to directly affecting the history of her family, America's use of the atomic bomb had been one of the most significant events in modern history. She decided to find out more about it.

Using Prewriting Techniques

In addition to conducting preliminary research, you may want to use one of the following prewriting techniques to help you come up with a specific topic:

1. **Freewriting and clustering.** Write whatever comes to mind about the subject for five minutes, or draw a cluster diagram in which you use lines to connect your subject with related ideas.

2. **Brainstorming.** Working with a group of friends or classmates, write down a list of topics that come to mind as people think about the subject.

3. **Questioning.** Write a list of questions about the subject. Begin each question with the word *who, what, where, when, why,* or *how,* or start your questions with *What if . . .*

4. **Discussing.** Listen to what other students know about your subject, what aspects of it they find intriguing, what difficulties they foresee in researching it, and so on.

Evaluating Possible Topics

Once you have generated a list of possible topic ideas, you need to evaluate them—that is, you need to judge them on the basis of certain criteria. Here are some criteria for judging a research topic:

1. **The topic should be interesting.** Often the most interesting topic is one that is related to your family's history, to your future, to your major goals, to the place where you live or would like to live, to a career that interests you, or to a hobby or other activity that you enjoy. The topic might be something that has caught your interest in the past, perhaps something you have read about or have studied in school.

2. **The topic should be covered in readily available sources.** When considering a topic, always check the catalogs of a couple of local libraries and the *Readers' Guide to Periodical Literature* to see if sources are available.

> "The topic might be something that has caught your interest in the past, perhaps something you have read about or have studied in school."

3. The topic should be significant. Choose a topic that is significant for you, one worth your time and energy.

4. The topic should be objective. Make sure that you will be able to gather enough facts about the topic to support your argument.

5. You should not simply rehash material available in other sources. You should look for a topic that allows you to establish a unique angle or approach.

6. The topic should be narrow enough to be treated fully. Ask your teacher how many pages long your paper should be, and choose a topic that is narrow enough to be treated in a paper of that length.

Writing a Statement of Controlling Purpose

" A statement of controlling purpose . . . controls, or guides, your research. "

Once you have decided on a specific topic, your next step is to write a **statement of controlling purpose.** This is a sentence or pair of sentences that tells what you want to accomplish in your paper. It is called a statement of controlling purpose because it controls, or guides, your research. The statement of controlling purpose usually contains one or more key words that tell what the paper is going to accomplish. Key words that often appear in statements of controlling purpose include *analyze, classify, compare, contrast, define, describe, determine, establish, explain, identify, prove,* and *support.*

Here are two examples of statements of controlling purpose:

> The purpose of this paper will be to analyze the impact of political demonstrations on U.S. policy during the Vietnam War.

> The purpose of this paper will be to contrast the leadership styles of President Harry S. Truman and Premier Joseph Stalin during the period 1945–1952.

To come up with a statement of controlling purpose, you will probably have to do a considerable amount of preliminary research. That is because before you can write a statement of controlling purpose, you need to know enough about your topic to have a general idea of what you want to say in your paper. Here is an example of one student's process.

One Student's Process: Sarah

Sarah was interested in learning more about the dropping of the atomic bomb in 1945. She knew that she wanted to focus more on the steps leading to the use of the bomb than on the event's aftermath. She began her research by reading encyclopedia entries on the atomic bomb. As she read, she wrote down key terms, including *Manhattan Project, Trinity,* and *Quebec Agreement.* She also wrote down the names of important people, such as Robert Oppenheimer, Leo Szilard, and President Harry S. Truman.

Sarah used these terms to search her library's computerized catalog. In this way, she found a number of books on the topic, including several firsthand accounts of the development of the bomb. In her preliminary reading she was struck that although in his memoirs Harry S. Truman claimed sole responsibility for the decision to drop the bomb, the story behind the decision seemed more complex than Truman's simple statement suggested. Sarah decided to write a paper that would explain the factors in the making of this momentous decision. Her statement of controlling purpose was "The purpose of this paper is to explain why the United States decided to drop the atomic bomb on Hiroshima."

> " To come up with a statement of controlling purpose, you will probably have to do a considerable amount of preliminary research. "

Here are some examples of types of controlling purpose:

Statements of Controlling Purpose

A controlling purpose can be to . . .

Support (or argue against) a policy: The purpose of this paper is to support the policy of limiting nuclear weapons that is expressed in the Nuclear Nonproliferation Treaty.

Prove (or refute) one or more statements of fact: The purpose of this paper is to prove that by failing to take action against Italy, the League of Nations was partly responsible for that country's takeover of Ethiopia in 1936.

Determine the relative values of two or more things: The purpose of this paper is to compare land-war tactics and air-war tactics to determine which type of warfare is more effective in a jungle war.

Analyze something into its parts and show how those parts relate to one another: The purpose of this paper is to describe the roles of various citizen groups and government agencies in the making of foreign policy.

Define something: The purpose of this paper is to define the phrase *freedom of the press* by explaining the nature of and the limits on press freedom under the law.

Explain causes or effects: The purpose of this paper is to explain the various economic causes of the destruction of Brazil's rain forests.

Establish a cause-effect relationship: The purpose of this paper is to present evidence suggesting that an increase in state and federal expenditure on education results in improved test scores.

Describe the development of something over time: The purpose of this paper is to describe how rock 'n' roll developed from roots in blues, gospel, and country music.

Identify and describe a general trend: The purpose of this paper is to show that a major extinction of South American plant and animal species is now occurring.

Classify individual items into groups or categories: The purpose of this paper is to classify African myths into several distinct categories (creation stories, lineage stories, etc.).

Relate a part to a whole: The purpose of this paper is to examine the Food Stamp Program as part of the federal government's welfare system in the 1970s.

Compare or contrast two things to show how they are similar or different: The purpose of this paper is to compare the tactics used by guerrillas in the Pacific theater during World War II with the tactics used by the Vietcong in the Vietnam War.

Examine a technique: The purpose of this paper is to examine persuasive techniques employed in World War II propaganda.

Explain a general concept by means of specific examples: The purpose of this paper is to explain the concept of multiple perspectives in history through examples of varied sources.

Explain the main idea or message of something: The purpose of this paper is to explain the political message of George Orwell's *1984.*

This list of types of controlling purpose is far from complete, so do not worry if the controlling purpose that you come up with does not fall into one of the categories in the list. Do bear in mind that your controlling purpose should be one that is significant to you and, potentially, to your readers.

Bear in mind as well that your controlling purpose may change as you do your research. When you begin writing your research paper, you will replace your controlling purpose with a **thesis statement,** a statement of your main idea. The thesis statement will not contain the phrase "the purpose of this paper is." For more information on writing thesis statements, see pages 85–86.

Finding and Recording Your Sources

Once you have written a statement of controlling purpose, you are ready to put together a list of potential sources. This list of sources that might be useful to you in writing your paper is called a **working bibliography.** You will already have used some sources during your preliminary research, and you will probably want to include some or all of those sources in your working bibliography. As you continue to research and draft, you may discover that some of the sources in this initial list are not useful, and you will undoubtedly find new sources to add to the list. Before you decide to add any source to your list, however, make sure to evaluate it. Information on how to evaluate a source can be found on pages 63–64. See pages 25–30 for a discussion of primary and secondary sources.

Both print and nonprint sources will be available to you, and you will want to take advantage of both. Here are some good places to start looking for information:

1. Other people. People can be a researcher's greatest resource. Consider interviewing a professor from a local college or university, or people who work for businesses, museums, historical societies, or other organizations.

2. Institutions and organizations. Museums, art galleries, state and local historical societies, and businesses are good sources of information about some topics. Many institutions and organizations maintain sites on the Internet.

3. The government. Many libraries have special departments that contain government publications. For some topics, you may want to contact town, city, county, state, or federal government offices directly. Listings of government departments and agencies can be found in telephone directories.

4. The library/media center. Remember that a library is more than just a place for housing books. Libraries also contain

> " People can be a researcher's greatest resource. "

periodicals—such as newspapers, magazines, and journals—and most have many nonprint materials, such as audiocassettes, videotapes, computer software, reproductions of artworks, and pamphlets. Many libraries also provide access to the Internet.

5. Bookstores. For some topics, the latest information can be found at your local bookstore. If you do not find what you are looking for, ask a bookstore employee to look up your subject or author in *Books in Print*.

6. Bibliographies. A **bibliography** is a list of books and other materials about a particular topic. Your reference librarian can point you to general bibliographies dealing with a variety of subjects, such as chemistry, the humanities, or plays by Shakespeare. You can also look for bibliographic lists in the backs of books about your topic.

7. On-line information services. An **on-line information service,** or **computer information service,** is an information source that can be communicated with by means of a personal computer and a modem. For information about on-line computer services, see Appendix A on pages 109–110.

8. Reference works. Reference works include almanacs, atlases, bibliographies, dictionaries, encyclopedias, periodical indexes, and thesauruses. You will find these and similar works in the reference department of your library.

9. Other sources. Do not neglect television programs, live theater performances, radio shows, recordings, videotapes, computer software, and other possible sources of information. Many libraries have extensive collections of audiovisual materials of all kinds, on a wide variety of subjects. Make use of these.

Evaluating Possible Sources

After you locate a potential source, you need to decide whether it will be useful to you. The following questions will help you to evaluate a source:

1. Is the source authoritative? An **authoritative source** is one that can be relied upon to provide accurate information.

Research Tip

Local and state government offices can often be useful to people who are doing historical research. For example, a county court clerk's office might be able to help you find copies of deeds, birth records, marriage records, and other such documents.

Consider the reputation of the publication and of the author. Are they well respected?

2. Is the source unbiased? An **unbiased source** is one whose author lacks any prejudices that might make his or her work unreliable. For example, the impartiality of a newsletter article claiming that there is no relationship between smoking and disease may be doubtful if the article is written by a lobbyist for a tobacco company.

3. Is it necessary for the source to be up-to-date? For some topics, such as ones associated with current events or with the impact of new technology, up-to-date sources are essential, so check the date on the copyright page of your source. For other topics, the copyright date may be less important or not important at all. If, for example, you were writing about 19th-century pioneer women in Wyoming, the old diaries and letters of such women would be excellent sources.

4. Is the work written at an appropriate level? Some materials are written for children and, although generally accurate, are simplified and may be misleading in some respects. Others are so technical that they can be understood only after years of study.

5. Does the source come highly recommended? One way to evaluate a source is to ask an expert or authority whether the source is reliable. You can also check the bibliography in a reputable source. If a source is listed in a bibliography, then it is probably considered reliable by the author or editor who put that bibliography together.

Preparing Bibliography Cards

Every time you find a source that may be useful for your research paper, you need to prepare a **bibliography card** for it. All of your bibliography cards, taken together, make up your **working bibliography.**

A bibliography card serves three basic purposes. First, it enables you to find the source again. Second, it enables you to prepare documentation for your paper. **Documentation** is mate-

Research Tip

If your topic involves recent events, current periodicals and journals are good sources of up-to-date information. If you have access to the Internet, you can also search it for up-to-date information. Remember, however, always to evaluate carefully the information you find on Internet sites.

rial included in a research paper to identify the sources from which information was taken. Third, it enables you to prepare the Works Cited list that will appear at the end of your paper. The **Works Cited list** is a complete record of the sources referred to in the paper. Here is a sample bibliography card.

Bibliography card for a book by a single author

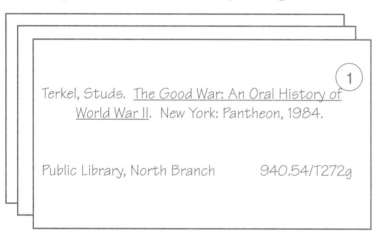

Terkel, Studs. *The Good War: An Oral History of World War II*. New York: Pantheon, 1984.

Public Library, North Branch   940.54/T272g

①

Research Tip

Works of art from a particular historical period are often useful primary sources. They can provide opportunities to examine the ways in which art reflects a particular society or the ways in which social conditions influence art.

Notice that a bibliography card contains all or most of the items described below.

1. A bibliographic entry gives essential information about a source, such as its author, its title, its place and/or date of publication, and the pages (of a book or magazine) on which it was found. The first line of the bibliographic entry begins in the upper left-hand corner of the card. Subsequent lines are indented a few spaces.

2. A source note tells where you found the source. The source listed above was found at the North Branch of the local public library. The source note will help you find the source again if you need to do so.

3. A source number should be written in the upper right-hand corner of the card and circled. Assign a different source number to each you find. You will use this number to refer to the source on any note cards containing material from that source.

4. A catalog number, if appropriate, should be included. Books and some other materials in libraries are assigned catalog numbers. If your source comes from a library and has a catalog number, you should write that number in the lower right-hand corner of the card. The catalog number will help you to find the source again if you need to do so.

Every time you find a possible source, follow these steps.

Evaluating and Recording Sources

1. Evaluate the source.

2. Select a blank 3″ × 5″ index card or slip of paper to use as a bibliography card.

3. Find the appropriate bibliographic form in Appendix C on pages 114–122. Then write on the bibliography card a complete bibliography entry for the source. Make sure you capitalize and punctuate the bibliography entry properly.

4. In the top right-hand corner of the card, record a source number and circle it.

5. At the bottom of the card, record the place where you found the source.

6. If the source has a catalog number, record that number as well.

7. Put the card with the stack of cards that make up your working bibliography.

Research Tip

You may want to look at literary works written during a historical period you are researching. They can give you a sense of the daily life and social attitudes of that time. Other useful primary sources are journals, collections of letters, and memoirs from the period under study.

Gathering Information

After you have written a statement of controlling purpose and have prepared a working bibliography, you are ready to begin gathering information for your paper. Begin with the most promising sources recorded on your bibliography cards—the ones that are the most general, the most authoritative, or the most accessible. Keeping your controlling purpose clearly in mind, start searching through your sources, looking for relevant information. Do not read, view, or listen to every part of every source. Concentrate on those parts that are relevant to your topic and your purpose.

Some nonprint sources, such as on-line encyclopedias, have indexes or special search features that will help you to find just those items of information that you need. If you conduct interviews as part of your research, you will be able to prepare questions beforehand to ensure that much of the information that you receive will be related to your topic and purpose.

Preparing Note Cards

There are three basic types of notes:

- A **direct quotation** repeats the words of a source exactly. Quotation marks are used around the quoted material.

- A **paraphrase** states an idea expressed by a source, but in different words.

- A **summary** is a condensation of an idea in a source. In other words, it says the same thing in fewer words.

Take notes on 4″ × 6″ cards. Use cards of that size to distinguish your note cards from your 3″ × 5″ bibliography cards. Use a separate card for each note so that you can rearrange your notes later on. As a rule of thumb, try to limit each note to one or two sentences on a single idea or subtopic. Focusing on one

> **"**Do not read, view, or listen to every part of every source. Concentrate on those parts that are relevant to your topic and your purpose.**"**

67

idea in each card makes it easier to group and reorganize the ideas later on.

When quoting, it is extremely important that you copy each letter and punctuation mark exactly. In paraphrasing or summarizing, you need to make sure that when you put the material into your own words, you do not change the source's meaning.

Give a page reference for any information taken from a source, except an entry in an encyclopedia or a dictionary.

- Information from a single page—write the page number after the note.

- Information from two or more consecutive pages—write the numbers of the first and last pages, as follows: 1–4. For consecutive numbers greater than 99, use only the last two digits of the second number, as follows: 110–15.

- Information from nonconsecutive pages in a periodical— write the number of the first page followed by a plus sign, as follows: 76+.

The following note card is well prepared. It is brief and deals with a single idea. The four main parts of the note card have been labeled.

Source number (Take this number from the appropriate bibliography card.)

Guideline (Keep cards with similar guidelines together.)

Note (This should be a quotation, a paraphrase, a summary, or a combination of those types of notes.)

Page reference (See instructions above.)

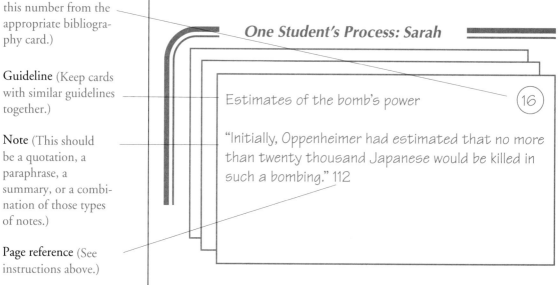

One Student's Process: Sarah

Estimates of the bomb's power   (16)

"Initially, Oppenheimer had estimated that no more than twenty thousand Japanese would be killed in such a bombing." 112

The following note card needs improvement. It presents two unrelated ideas.

Deciding surrender terms for Japan / Dealing ⑫
with the USSR

After the successful bomb test, Byrnes felt, "With
such weapons in the U.S. arsenal, unconditional
surrender need not be compromised. And America
no longer required the Soviet Union's aid in the
Pacific." 686

This note comes from one page of one source, but it contains two ideas that are only distantly related to one another. The writer needs to place these ideas on two separate note cards.

The material on this card should be recorded on two separate cards.

When recording a direct quotation, you may wish to add an explanatory note to identify the speaker or to provide necessary background information. Such an explanatory note can be a summary or a paraphrase. The following note card, for example, contains a summary that provides a context for the quoted material.

Reasons for starting bomb research ⑤

Albert Einstein warned President Franklin D.
Roosevelt in 1939 that atomic bombs could be
made from uranium. He wrote, "A single bomb of
this type, carried by boat and exploded in a port,
might very well destroy the whole port together
with some of the surrounding territory." 1

This note begins with a summary that introduces a quotation. Many of your notes will combine quotations with summaries or paraphrases.

The chart on the next page explains when to use the various types of notes.

When to Quote, Paraphrase, and Summarize

1. **Direct quotation.** Use a direct quotation when an idea is especially well stated in a source—that is, when a passage is notable for its succinctness, its clarity, its liveliness, its elegance of expression, or some other exceptional quality. Also use a direct quotation when the exact wording is important historically, legally, or as a matter of definition.

2. **Paraphrase.** Use the paraphrase as your basic note form—the form that you always use unless you have a good reason to quote or summarize your source.

3. **Summary.** Use a summary when a passage in a source is too long to be succinctly quoted or paraphrased.

4. **Quotation plus summary or paraphrase.** Write this kind of note when the exact words of the source are desirable but require some explanation to be clear, to be properly attributed, or to be identified as fact or opinion.

The following guidelines will help you to improve your note-taking skills.

Effective Note Taking

1. Keep your topic, controlling purpose, and audience in mind at all times. Do not record material unrelated to your topic.

2. Make sure that summaries and paraphrases accurately express the ideas in your sources.

Effective Note Taking (cont.)

3. Be accurate. Make sure that direct quotations are reproduced word for word, with capitalization, spelling, grammar, and punctuation precisely as in the original. Make sure that every direct quotation begins and ends with quotation marks.

4. Double-check statistics and facts to make sure that you have them right.

5. Distinguish between fact and opinion by labeling opinions as such: "Dr. Graves thinks that . . ." or "According to Grace Jackson . . ."

6. Nonessential parts of a quotation can be cut if the overall meaning of the quotation is not changed. Indicate omissions from quotations by using **points of ellipsis,** a series of three spaced dots (. . .). Simply use the three dots when cutting material within a sentence. Use a period before the dots (. . . .) when cutting a full sentence, a paragraph, or more than a paragraph. Also use a period before the dots when you cut material from the end of a sentence.

7. Always double-check page references. It's easy to copy these incorrectly.

Research Tip

When dealing with facts and statistics,
1. Always double-check them to make sure that you are transcribing them accurately.
2. When possible, check them in at least two different sources.
3. Use sources that are well respected and authoritative.

Avoiding Plagiarism

One of the purposes of using a working bibliography and note cards is to help you to avoid plagiarism. **Plagiarism** is the act of intentionally or unintentionally presenting work done by someone else as though it were your own. In most schools, including high schools and universities, plagiarism is considered a serious offense and can result in severe penalties, such as failing grades, loss of course credit, or even expulsion.

Because plagiarism is so serious, it is important to know exactly what it is and what you can do to avoid it. Here is a simple test to determine whether something is plagiarized: ask yourself, Is this information, idea, or statement common knowledge? If the answer is no, then ask yourself, Did this information, idea, or statement come from a source outside myself, or did it come from my own experience or as a result of my own creative activity? If the information, idea, or statement is not common knowledge, and if it came from an outside source, then you must credit that source. Failure to do so constitutes plagiarism.

Developing a Preliminary Outline

At some point early in your research, you will come to know enough about your topic to begin to develop a **preliminary,** or rough, **outline.** A preliminary outline is useful because it will help you to focus your search for information. The preliminary outline should list some key ideas or subtopics that you expect to include in the body of your paper. As you learn more about your topic, your preliminary outline will change and grow, but even a short, incomplete preliminary outline can be useful.

One Student's Process: Sarah

Soon after Sarah began her research on the steps leading to the dropping of the bomb, she decided that it would be best to organize her paper chronologically. Rather than writing a complete outline, she grouped her ideas into three main categories:

> Background
> —scientific research
> —World War II
> Early development of the bomb
> —Manhattan Project
> —Quebec Agreement
> Completion of the bomb
> —debate about using bomb
> —final decision to use bomb

> " If the information, idea, or statement is not common knowledge, and if it came from an outside source, then you must credit that source. Failure to do so constitutes plagiarism. "

A preliminary outline can consist of a few entries or of many. In a preliminary outline, main entries are usually begun at the left-hand margin, and subentries are introduced by dashes.

The Note Taking/Outlining Cycle

Writing is a cyclical process. At any point in the process, you can stop what you are doing and return to an earlier point. For example, you might decide after doing a bit of research to return to the very beginning and to choose a new topic, or you might decide to change your statement of controlling purpose. In other words, you are free to return to the beginning and to start the writing cycle all over again.

Nowhere in the process of preparing a research paper is the cyclical nature of writing more apparent than in the stage in which you gather information. During this stage, you will continually go back and forth between your preliminary outline and your note cards. As you do more research and take more notes, you will acquire more and more information that you can use to improve your outline. As you change the headings in your outline, you will want to reorganize your note cards, to change the guidelines on the note cards, and to take new notes related to your outline's headings. Your notes and your outline will grow and change together—each one feeding into the other.

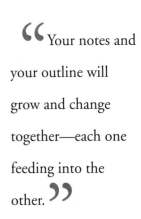

"Your notes and your outline will grow and change together—each one feeding into the other."

Organizing Your Material

In the preceding chapter you learned that writing a research paper is a cyclical process. The more research you do, and the more information you gather on note cards, the more you will understand your topic. The more you understand your topic, the more detailed you can make your preliminary outline. The more detailed your preliminary outline becomes, the more you will understand what additional information you need to gather.

At first your preliminary outline will probably be sketchy. However, over time it will become quite detailed. To develop a detailed outline, you will need to consider, over and over again, how best to organize the information that you are gathering. Of course, as you write and research, the organization can and probably will change.

Organizing Ideas in a Research Paper

Much of the writing that people do is fiction, how-to writing, or personal correspondence, and almost all of this writing is organized chronologically. Other writing, including a great deal of nonfiction, is usually organized not in any one way but in what might be called **part-by-part order.** One idea or group of ideas suggests another, which suggests another, and so on to the end. Each idea is related in some way to the one that precedes it and to the one that follows it, but no single, overall method of organization is used.

There are even more possible ways to organize research papers than there are possible topics for such papers. Consequently, there are no hard-and-fast rules about how ideas in research papers should be organized. However, here are some guidelines to keep in mind:

1. Your paper will begin with an introduction that states your thesis. It will end with a conclusion that restates your thesis

"A great deal of nonfiction is usually organized not in any one way but in what might be called part-by-part order. One idea or group of ideas suggests another, which suggests another, and so on to the end.**"**

and that summarizes the main point or points of the paper. You need to concentrate on organizing the body of the paper. Your goal is to find a sensible method of arranging the evidence that you will present in the body.

2. Many topics require that you start by providing background information. If you have chosen such a topic, think about what essential background information should appear early on, and group that information together. You might want to include among this background information definitions of any key terms that will appear in your paper.

3. Remember that events are usually presented in chronological order, unless there is a good reason to present them in some other way. So if part or all of your paper involves presenting events, consider organizing those events chronologically.

4. As you gather your notes, or evidence, sort the note cards into separate piles of related ideas and information. Try different combinations, and make rough outlines based on them.

5. Once you have your note cards separated into piles of related ideas and information, come up with a phrase to describe what is in each pile. Think about the different orders in which you could present each group of ideas. Should the ideas in pile one be presented first, or those in pile three? Why?

6. Look for relationships between the ideas and information in each group of note cards. Also look for relationships between groups of cards. The following chart describes some of the relationships that you might discover.

Ways to Relate Ideas

1. **Chronological order:** from first event to last event or from last event to first event

2. **Spatial order:** by arrangement in space

3. **Classification:** in groups sharing similar properties or characteristics

Ways to Relate Ideas (cont.)

4. **Order of degree:** according to importance, value, interest, obviousness, certainty, or similar quality

5. **Cause-and-effect order:** from cause to effect or from effect to cause

6. **Comparison-and-contrast order:** with similarities followed by differences or differences followed by similarities

7. **Analytical order:** according to parts and the relationships between the parts

8. **Inductive order, or synthesis:** with specific examples followed by generalization from those examples

9. **Deductive order:** with a general idea or principle followed by specific conclusions drawn from that general idea or principle

10. **Order of impression, or association:** according to the sequence in which things strike one's attention

11. **Hierarchical order:** from class to subclass (group within a class) or vice versa

Research Tip

Many history research papers are organized chronologically. However, research papers on topics in social studies often involve explaining why something occurred or occurs, so the writers of such papers often also make use of cause-and-effect order, at least in part.

Creating a Draft Outline

Before beginning your rough draft, you will want to create a draft outline. A **draft outline** is a formal outline that is used as the basis for a rough draft. It can be a **sentence outline,** containing entries that are all complete sentences, or it can be a **topic outline,** containing entries that are words, phrases, or clauses.

A draft outline begins with a statement of controlling purpose. It is divided into two or more major sections introduced by Roman numerals (I, II). Each major section is divided into two or more subsections introduced by capital letters (A, B). The subsections may be divided into sub-subsections introduced by Arabic numerals (1, 2), and those into sub-sub-subsections introduced by lowercase letters (a, b).

One Student's Process: Sarah

Sarah wrote a draft outline for her paper on the decision to drop the atomic bomb. She chose to produce a topic outline:

Topic Outline

```
                The Road to Hiroshima
Controlling Purpose: The purpose of this
paper is to show that although President
Harry Truman claimed sole responsibility for
the dropping of atomic bombs on Japan, the
story behind the decision to use the bomb is
far more complex than Truman's simple state-
ment suggests. A number of people were
involved in the decision, and their deliber-
ations involved a number of ethical,
political, and military issues.
  I.   Scientific and historical background
       A. Physics discoveries: nuclear struc-
          ture and nuclear fission
       B. World War II
       C. Atomic-bomb research
          1. Why national leaders wanted
             atomic-bomb research
          2. Why scientists participated
          3. A turning point: creating a
             nuclear pile
 II.   Atomic bomb development
       A. Organization of the Manhattan
          Project
       B. The Quebec Agreement
III.   Atomic bomb completion: complications
       and final decisions
```

When preparing a formal outline for submission to a teacher or to a peer reviewer, always double-space the outline. On the first page of the outline, include your name, your teacher's name, the name of your class, and the date, as shown in the sample research paper on page 5 of this book. Then, on subsequent pages, if there are any, include your last name and the page number in the upper right-hand corner.

A. Niels Bohr's warnings to Roosevelt and Churchill
B. Unexpected events and their effects
   1. V-E Day
   2. Roosevelt's death
C. The final decision process
   1. The Interim Committee and the Target Committee
   2. Leo Szilard's warnings to Truman
   3. The Alamogordo test and the Potsdam conference
D. Final events leading up to the bombing of Japan
   1. Advance military preparations for the bombing
   2. The Potsdam Declaration and Japan's response

You could add a conclusion to the end of your outline, stating the main point that you wish to make in the research paper.

Here is how the first four entries might look if this were a sentence outline:

I. Scientific discoveries and historical events of the 1920s, 1930s, and 1940s laid the groundwork for the development and use of the atomic bomb.
   A. In physics, the discoveries of nuclear structure and nuclear fission suggested the possibility of an atomic bomb.
   B. The outbreak of World War II provided additional motivation for the development of an atomic bomb.
   C. By 1940, government-funded atomic-bomb research was under way.

Drafting Your Research Paper

After completing a draft outline and arranging your note cards to match the outline, you are ready to begin writing your rough draft. The comforting thing about a rough draft is that it does not have to be perfect. You can rework your draft as often as you like and watch it take shape gradually. In other words, you do not have to hit a home run your first time at bat. You can have as many chances at the plate as you want.

Approaches to Drafting

With regard to drafting, writers fall into two major camps. Some prefer to get everything down on paper quickly, but in very rough form, and then do one or more detailed revisions. Others like to complete each section as they go, writing and polishing one section, then moving on to the next. Either approach is acceptable. If you choose the second approach, however, you might want to look first at pages 89–94, on revision.

The Style of the Draft

A research paper is an example of objective, formal writing. Therefore, you should avoid making the paper personal and subjective, and you should avoid using informal language. Do not use such words as *I, me, my, mine, we,* and *our.* Do not state opinions without supporting them with facts. Do not use slang, colloquialisms, nonstandard dialect, or contractions. Avoid referring to your paper except when summarizing its contents.

Assembling the Draft

A rough draft is just that—it is rough, or unfinished. As you draft, do not worry about matters that you can take care of later,

> " You do not have to hit a home run your first time at bat. You can have as many chances at the plate as you want. "

such as the details of spelling, grammar, usage, and mechanics. Instead, concentrate on getting your ideas down in an order that makes sense.

Use your outline as a guide. Explore each main point, supporting the idea with evidence from your note cards. When you use information from a note card, include the source number from the note card in your draft and circle it. Noting the source number is extremely important because during revision you will have to find the source in order to document it.

❝ Use your outline as a guide. Explore each main point, supporting the idea with evidence from your note cards. ❞

━━━ *One Student's Process: Sarah* ━━━

One of the entries in Sarah's outline for her paper on the atomic bomb was the following:

```
Why scientists participated
```

Sarah turned this entry into a statement, which she used as a topic sentence:

```
Scientists participated in the bomb
project for a variety of reasons.
```

Then she added material from her note cards to support the topic sentence.

```
      Scientists already conducting fission
research were asked to participate in the
U.S. and British bomb projects. Some
accepted for practical reasons; others,
for scientific reasons. As Teller
explained in a later interview, "I
believe that . . . scientists have the
responsibility of developing tools for
mankind" (16) . In addition, many of the
scientists were refugees from Nazi and
Fascist brutality.
```

Notice that Sarah added quoted material to support the topic sentence. She included a source number from a note card so that she would be able to find that source later on, when she was preparing the documentation, or full source information, for her paper.

Incorporating summaries and paraphrases. Working summaries and paraphrases into your paper is quite easy. Simply write them out as part of your text and include a source number at the end of the summarized or paraphrased material. Just be certain that transitions connect the material smoothly to what precedes or follows it.

Incorporating quotations. Working quotations into your paper is a bit more complicated because there are many ways in which quotations can be used. Also, the rules for prose differ from those for poetry or song lyrics. See the chart on pages 82–83 for complete instructions on using quotations in your draft.

The Draft as a Work in Progress

Occasionally, as you write, you may discover gaps in the information that you have gathered. In other words, you may find that you do not have in your note cards all the information you need to make some point. When that occurs, you can stop and look for the information, or you can simply make a note to yourself to find the information later on. Either approach is acceptable.

The need to fill gaps is one example of a general characteristic of drafting: that drafting is still discovery time. In addition to discovering gaps to be filled, you may discover better ways to organize parts of the paper, contradictions in your source materials, or significant parts of your topic that you have not yet explored. You may even find a whole new approach to your topic, one more interesting or workable than the one you have taken. Remain open to these developments—to the discoveries that occur as you draft. Be willing to return to previous stages of the writing process, if necessary, to do more research, to rethink your controlling purpose, or to change your outline.

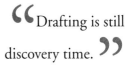

"Drafting is still discovery time."

Quoting Prose Works

1. If a quotation is four lines long or less, put it in quotation marks and place it in the text of your paper:

    ```
    Truman wrote in his memoirs, "The final decision of
    where and when to use the bomb was up to me."(2).
    ```

    Of course, the circled number is the source number from your note card. When you do your final documentation, this number will be replaced with a citation in parentheses. (See pages 95–102.)

2. You do not have to quote complete sentences:

    ```
    Truman wrote in his memoirs that the responsibility
    for "the final decision of where and when to use the
    bomb" was his alone (2).
    ```

3. You can also break a quotation into two parts:

    ```
    "The final decision of where and when to use the bomb,"
    wrote Truman in his memoirs, "was up to me"(2).
    ```

4. When a quoted passage is more than four lines long, set it off from the text of your paper. Put a colon after the statement that introduces the quotation. Begin a new line. Indent the entire quotation ten spaces from the left-hand margin. Double-space the quotation, and do not enclose it in quotation marks:

    ```
    In a letter to President Franklin D. Roosevelt,
    Albert Einstein issued this warning:
              This new phenomenon would also lead to the
              construction of bombs, and it is conceivable
              . . . that extremely powerful bombs of a new
              type may thus be constructed. A single bomb
              of this type, carried by boat and exploded
              in a port, might very well destroy the whole
              port together with some of the surrounding
              territory.(5)
    ```

5. When quoting more than one paragraph, indent the first line of each full paragraph an additional three spaces. However, indent the first sentence only if it begins a paragraph in your source.

Quoting Prose Works (cont.)

```
In the next month, the Interim Committee debated ethi-
cal and practical aspects of the use of the bomb, as
Byrnes recalled:
          Then there was a question of giving the
          Japanese fair warning about the time and place
          of the explosion, but we rejected it because
          we feared the American prisoners of war would
          be brought into the designated area. We were
          told by experts, too, that . . . they could
          not guarantee that . . . [the] bomb would
          explode when dropped. . . .
             If we gave the Japanese advance notice of
          the time and place we would drop the bomb,
          and then the bomb failed to explode, . . .
          Japanese militarists . . . would say that our
          failure was proof that we were merely bluffing
          about possessing the bomb. (12)
```

Quoting Poetry, Verse Plays, and Songs

1. When quoting a single line or part of a line, simply place the material in your text with quotation marks around it:

```
Shakespeare's Macbeth says, "Life's but a walking
shadow"( 4 ).
```

2. When quoting two or three lines, separate the lines with a space, a slash (/), and another space:

```
Shakespeare's Macbeth says: "Life's but a walking
shadow, a poor player, / That struts and frets his hour
upon the stage / And then is heard no more"( 4 ).
```

When quoting four or more lines, set the material off from your text. Indent it ten spaces, double-space it, and do not enclose it in quotation marks. Follow the line division and spacing of the original.

Using Graphic Aids

As you draft, stay alert to the possibility of using tables, maps, charts, diagrams, and other **graphic aids** to present information concisely. If you use a graphic aid from a source, or if you use information from a source to create a graphic aid, then you must credit the source of the information.

Tables should be labeled "Table 1," "Table 2," and so on. Other graphic aids should be labeled "Fig. 1," "Fig. 2," and so on. Place the label after the figure and follow it with a caption that is either the title of the graphic aid or a description of the graphic aid. Follow that with a source credit in endnote form.

One Student's Process: Marcus

Marcus was doing a paper on the attack of the African-American Massachusetts 54th Infantry Regiment on the Confederate stronghold of Fort Wagner, South Carolina, during the Civil War. His completed paper is on pages 136 – 142. Here is a graphic that Marcus created, based on a map that he found while doing his research:

Fig. 1. Charleston harbor, 1863. Adapted from Peter Burchard, <u>One Gallant Rush: Robert Gould Shaw and His Brave Black Regiment</u> (New York: St. Martin's, 1965) 110.

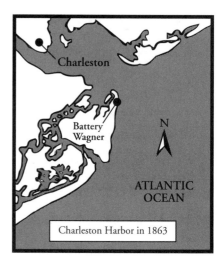

Charleston

Battery Wagner

N

ATLANTIC OCEAN

Charleston Harbor in 1863

Writing the Introduction

The introduction to a research paper should accomplish two purposes:

1. It should grab your readers' attention.

2. It should present the paper's main idea, or **thesis statement.**

In addition, the introduction may define key terms, supply necessary background information, or both. The introduction can be of any length, although most introductions are one or two paragraphs long.

Capturing the Reader's Attention

There are many ways to capture readers' attention in an introduction. You can begin with a startling or unusual fact, with a question, with an anecdote (a brief story that makes a point), with an analogy (a comparison between the topic and something with which readers are already familiar), with a paragraph that compares or contrasts, or with examples.

Writing the Thesis Statement

To create your thesis statement, you can simply recast your statement of controlling purpose. You may decide to change the statement, however, to reflect any additional refining or refocusing of your topic that has occurred during research. In either case, avoid using the phrase "the purpose of this paper" in your final thesis statement. Notice how that phrase is eliminated in the following example.

```
Controlling Purpose: The purpose of this
paper is to show that although President
Harry Truman claimed sole responsibility
for the dropping of atomic bombs on Japan,
the story behind the decision to use the
bomb is far more complex than Truman's
simple statement suggests. A number of
people were involved in the decision, and
```

> "The introduction to a research paper should . . . grab your readers' attention [and] . . . present the paper's main idea, or thesis statement."

85

their deliberations involved a number of
ethical, political, and military issues.

Thesis Statement: Although President Harry
Truman claimed sole responsibility for the
dropping of atomic bombs on Japan, the
story behind the decision to use the bomb
is far more complex than his simple statement suggests. A number of people were
involved in the decision, and their deliberations involved a number of ethical,
political, and military issues.

Sometimes, in order for your readers to understand your thesis statement, you will have to provide some additional
background information. In an introduction you need provide
only enough information to make it possible for them to understand the thesis statement. You can provide additional
information, as necessary, in the body of your paper.

One Student's Process: Marcus

Marcus's thesis statement for his paper on the
Massachusetts 54th Infantry Regiment was "Although
many Yankee soldiers lost their lives in the charge on
Fort Wagner, and although the Confederates technically
won the battle, the charge of the Massachusetts 54th was
a great victory for the North and for the antislavery
movement." Since some readers may never have heard of
the Massachusetts 54th or of Fort Wagner, Marcus
decided to open with some background information:

On July 18, 1863, at the height of the
Civil War, the men of the African-American
Massachusetts 54th Infantry attacked a South
Carolina earthwork known as Fort Wagner or
Battery Wagner. When the fighting was done,
nearly half of those men lay dead in what

was by all accounts a massacre, an overwhelming victory for the Confederacy⑧.
However, the African-American soldiers of
the 54th had fought as free men. So although
many of these Yankee soldiers lost their
lives in the charge, and although the
Confederates technically won the battle,
the charge of the Massachusetts 54th was
a moral, if not a military, victory for
the North and for the antislavery movement.

One Student's Process: Sarah

In her introduction, Sarah wanted to accomplish two purposes: she wanted to provide a historical context for her paper, and she wanted to state her thesis, or main idea. She decided to begin with some basic facts about the dropping of the atomic bombs in 1945. She also wanted to mention the effect of this event on international relations.

In August 1945, after three and a half
brutal years of participation in World War
II, the United States dropped atomic bombs
on Hiroshima and Nagasaki, Japan. The bombs
ended the war, but the cost was higher than
anyone had foreseen. Hundreds of thousands
of civilians were killed by the blasts and
the effects of radiation⑤. Almost at once,
a deadly nuclear-arms race began.

87

Then, in the last two sentences of her second paragraph, Sarah introduced her thesis statement:

```
    Why did the United States take such a
drastic step? President Harry S. Truman
later accepted full responsibility. "The
final decision of where and when to use the
bomb," he maintained in his memoirs, "was up
to me" ②. Yet the bombing of Japan was any-
thing but a one-person decision. The story
behind the decision to use the bomb is far
more complex than Truman's simple statement
suggests. A number of people were involved
in the decision to use the atomic bomb, and
their deliberations involved a number of
ethical, political, and military issues.
```

Writing the Conclusion

Like an introduction, a conclusion is usually one or two paragraphs long. The most common way to conclude a research paper is to restate the main idea and the principal arguments presented to support that idea. In addition, you may wish to use the conclusion to tie up any loose ends left in the body of your paper, to explain consequences of accepting the truth of the thesis statement, to call on the reader to take some action, to explain the importance or value of what the reader has learned from the paper, or to make predictions about the future. The conclusion is an opportunity to be imaginative. Almost anything is acceptable as long as the reader is left with a satisfactory sense that the treatment of the subject has been completed. (See the sample conclusions on pages 49 and 139–140 of this book.)

> **"** The conclusion is an opportunity to be imaginative. Almost anything is acceptable as long as the reader is left with a satisfactory sense that the treatment of the subject has been completed. **"**

Revising Your Research Paper

After you finish drafting your research paper, put it aside for a day or so. Distancing yourself from the paper will help you to view it more objectively in preparation for revising it.

Expect the revision of your paper to take several days, and expect to revise your paper more than once. One excellent approach is to do separate revisions for content and organization, for style, and for documentation. During revision, do not worry about the details of spelling, grammar, usage, and mechanics. You can clean up problems in those areas later on, during the proofreading stage. With regard to documentation, all you have to worry about at this point is having a source number in your manuscript for every instance in which you have used a source. The next chapter will explain how to turn the source numbers into complete, final documentation.

Peer Response

At some point during the drafting process, give your paper to one of your peers, or fellow students, for review. By having a peer review your paper, you can find out whether you've fulfilled your purpose, whether you have been completely clear, what parts cause problems for readers, and so on.

Do not worry about losing control of your work. You have the right to accept or reject any suggestions that your peer reviewer makes. Here are some questions you can ask your peer reviewer to elicit useful responses from him or her.

Questions for Peer Readers

- What do you think my main point, or thesis, is? Do you think I have proved that point? Why or why not? What could I do to make the proof more complete?

- Which sections of the paper did you find most interesting or informative?

- Were any parts of the paper unclear to you?

- What questions do you have about my topic now that you have read my paper? Were any important topic-related questions left unanswered?

Self-Evaluation

A peer reviewer's comments can give you important insights into how a paper can be improved. However, it is also important that you conduct your own close evaluation of the paper. Ask yourself the questions on the following checklist.

Revision Checklist

CONTENT AND ORGANIZATION

General

☐ **1.** Does your paper adequately support or prove the thesis statement?

☐ **2.** Does your paper have a clear introduction, body, and conclusion?

☐ **3.** Does every idea follow logically from the one that precedes it?

☐ **4.** Have you used transitions throughout to show the connections between ideas?

Introduction

☐ **5.** Will the introduction capture your readers' attention?

☐ **6.** Does the introduction present your thesis statement clearly?

Body

☐ **7.** Does the body of your paper present evidence from a wide variety of reliable sources?

☐ **8.** Is information from your sources presented in a combination of summary, paraphrase, and quotation?

☐ **9.** Are there any gaps in your argument that should be filled by doing additional research? Are there any points that are inadequately supported?

☐ **10.** Has all unnecessary or irrelevant material been deleted from the body of your paper?

☐ **11.** Have you avoided unsubstantiated statements of opinion throughout?

Conclusion

☐ **12.** Did you restate your thesis in the conclusion of your paper?

☐ **13.** Does your conclusion summarize the main points that you have presented in support of the thesis?

☐ **14.** Does your conclusion give your readers a satisfactory sense of completion? (Are all the loose ends tied up? Have all the parts of the thesis been supported? Have all of readers' most likely questions about the topic been addressed?)

STYLE

☐ **15.** Have you achieved variety by using many kinds of sentences—short and long sentences; simple, compound, complex, and compound-complex sentences; declarative, exclamatory, and interrogative sentences; and sentences that begin with different parts of speech?

☐ **16.** Have you avoided wordiness? Have you deleted unnecessary words, phrases, and clauses?

☐ **17.** Have you used clear, concrete examples? Have you defined key terms?

18. Have you avoided colloquial language, slang, jargon, and dialect? Have you avoided contractions, personal references, and first-person pronouns such as *I, we, me,* and *our* throughout?

19. Are the sentences in the paper graceful and not awkward?

DOCUMENTATION

20. Have you avoided plagiarism by completely documenting all materials taken from sources? Does every summary, paraphrase, or quotation have a corresponding source number?

21. Is each of your direct quotations set off by quotation marks or by indention? Is each quotation accurate? Does it reflect precisely what was in the source from which it was taken?

22. Is there a complete bibliography card, in proper form, for every source number in the final version of your manuscript? (For information on proper bibliography form, see pages 114–122.)

One Student's Process: Sarah

Sarah wrote a rough draft of her paper on the steps leading to the dropping of the atomic bomb. Then she revised the draft for content and organization. In one paragraph, she added information to given an example of a military target. She replaced the pronoun *it* with a noun to clarify what she was writing about. She moved a sentence to improve the paragraph's organization, and she cut a sentence that was irrelevant to this section of the research paper.

As scientists described the power of the bomb and the effects of the radiation it would release on impact, the committee members sat stunned. Stimson felt that, if ~~it~~ the bomb were used at all, it would have to be a "precision style" bombing of a military target, such as a weapons plant, to spare human lives. To ~~Byrnes~~ him, quickly getting ahead of the Soviet Union in the race seemed the only defense, since ". . . so far as the Soviet Union is concerned, they respect power (12). ~~He~~ Byrnes considered an idea with horror he had previously considered completely impossible—that the USSR might soon develop an atomic bomb of its own to use. ~~This concern echoed Truman's and Churchill's alarm at Stalin's increasingly aggressive policies.~~

Then Sarah revised her paragraph for style. She deleted unnecessary words, reordered a sentence to correct a misplaced modifier ("with horror"), and replaced the phrase "getting ahead . . . in the race" with a less vague phrase.

Finally, Sarah fixed any remaining problems in her documentation. She added a missing source number and some missing quotation marks, and she fixed a sentence that she had quoted inaccurately, adding a word that she had accidentally dropped. When she proofread the final version of her paper, Sarah corrected the remaining errors in spelling, grammar, and mechanics. Compare the revised paragraph on the preceding page with Sarah's final version on page 44 of this book.

Preparing a Final Outline

Your teacher may ask you to submit a final outline along with the final draft of your paper. If so, revise the last version of your draft outline, making sure to follow the guidelines for outlining given on pages 76–78. In most cases either a topic outline or a sentence outline is acceptable, though your teacher may prefer one type of outline over the other. The final outline should be typed or prepared on a word processor. For information on proper manuscript form for the outline and for the rest of the paper, see pages 106–107 of this book.

Documenting Your Sources

Each time you use information from your note cards, write down a source number. After you revise your draft, use the source numbers in the revised draft to prepare your documentation. **Documentation** is the information in the paper that tells what sources you used.

Parenthetical Documentation

The method of documentation most widely used today is called **parenthetical documentation.** This method has largely replaced the use of endnotes or footnotes for documentation. (For information on endnotes, footnotes, and other alternative methods of documentation, see Appendix D on pages 123–143.)

To acknowledge a source by means of parenthetical documentation, enclose a brief reference in parentheses. The reference, which is called a **parenthetical citation,** usually consists of an author's name and a page number:

```
Henry Stimson felt that if the bomb were used
at all, it would have to be used in a "preci-
sion-style" bombing of a military target, such
as a weapons plant, to spare human lives
(Rhodes 650).
```

The process of placing the citation into your text is called **citing a source.**

A parenthetical citation contains just enough information to help the reader locate the source in the Works Cited list at the end of the paper. The Works Cited list consists of bibliographic entries like those in Appendix C on pages 114–122.

Take a moment to look at the sample research paper on pages 37–51. Study the examples of parenthetical citations throughout the paper. Then look at the Works Cited list on pages 50–51, at the end of the sample paper.

Preparing Parenthetical Citations

Preparing parenthetical citations to document your sources is fairly straightforward, and by creating them you make your sources easily accessible to your readers. The following guidelines will help you to cite your sources properly:

1. Basic citation. Place the citation at the end of the sentence that contains the material being documented. The citation should appear after the text of the sentence but before the end mark:

```
They alerted the governments of the United
States and Britain (Clark 109).
```

2. Basic citation with author's name in text. If the name of the author is clear from the context in which the parenthetical citation appears, then give only the page number:

```
As Teller explained in a later interview,
"I believe that . . . scientists have the respon-
sibility of developing tools for mankind" (76).
```

3. Citation of a long quotation. When documenting a long quotation that is set off from the text, place the citation after the end punctuation:

```
In a letter to President Franklin D.
Roosevelt, Albert Einstein issued this warning:
        This new phenomenon would also lead
        to the construction of bombs, and it
        is conceivable . . . that extremely
        powerful bombs of a new type may
        thus be constructed. A single bomb
        of this type, carried by boat and
        exploded in a port, might very well
```

" Preparing parenthetical citations . . . is fairly straightforward, and by creating them you make your sources easily accessible to your readers. "

```
destroy the whole port together with some of

the surrounding territory.(1)
```

4. Citation of multiple works by one author. If the Works Cited list contains more than one work by the author, then include a shortened version of the title. When shortening a title, drop any small opening word like *a, an,* or *the;* begin with the word that the full title is alphabetized by; and reduce the overall length to one to four words. So, for example, the title "A Petition to the President of the United States" might become "Petition":

```
By July 17, Szilard had prepared a petition

that asked Truman not to use the bomb "without

seriously considering the moral responsibili-

ties which are involved" ("Petition").
```

5. Citation with author's name and title in text. If the name of the author and the title of the work both appear in the text of your paper, use only the page number, even if more than one work by the author is listed in your Works Cited list:

```
In the first volume of his memoirs, entitled

Year of Decisions, Truman maintained, "The final

decision of where and when to use the bomb was

up to me" (419).
```

6. Citation of a work available in various editions. When citing a literary work available in a variety of editions, include information that will allow readers to find the quotation in any edition. For a novel, include a chapter number:

```
Concern about the destructive power of this new

weapon was reflected in much postwar literature.

In his dystopian vision of the future, for

example, George Orwell wrote, that "atomic

bombs first appeared as early as the Nineteen-

forties, and were first used on a large scale

about ten years later" (1984 160; ch. 9).
```

For a short story or essay, include a paragraph number: (Donne, "Meditation 17" 300; par. 7). For a play divided into acts and scenes, give the act number and the scene number, separated by a period. Omit the page number(s). If the play is a well-known classic, the author's name can be omitted as well: (Macbeth 5.5).

7. Citation of an anonymous work. When citing an anonymous work (one for which no author is given), give the title or a shortened version of the title, followed by the page number if appropriate. Make sure that the first word in a shortened version of a title is the word by which the work is alphabetized in the Works Cited list:

```
Hundreds of thousands of civilians were killed
by the blasts and the effects of radiation
("World War II").
```

8. Citation of an encyclopedia or a similar reference work. When citing an article in a reference work that is arranged alphabetically—an encyclopedia or a biographical dictionary, for example—give only the title or a shortened version of the title:

```
The first bomb was exploded 120 miles south of
Albuquerque on July 16, 1945 ("Manhattan
Project").
```

9. Citation of a work by two or three authors. When citing a work by two or three authors, give the authors' last names and the page number:

```
One of Churchill's first thoughts at the news
was that the Allies could avoid the great num-
bers of casualties expected in the Pacific
theater (Le Vien and Lord 384).
```

10. Citation of a work by more than three authors. When citing a work by more than three authors, give the last name of the first author, followed by *et al.* and the page number. *Et al.* is an abbreviation of Latin *et alii,* or *et aliae,* meaning "and others":

```
The committee urged that Japan be given a harm-
less demonstration of an atomic explosion
(Franck et al.).
```

11. Citation of a quotation appearing in a source. When citing a statement that is quoted by your source, use the abbreviation *qtd. in:*

```
They also formulated the Potsdam Declaration,
demanding Japan's immediate "unconditional sur-
render" and threatening "prompt and utter
destruction" if Japan failed to comply (qtd. in
Rhodes 692).
```

12. Citation of a nonpaginated source. If the source is something that does not have page numbers—an interview, a piece of computer software, or a recording, for example—give the name of the author or interviewee. If there is no name, give the title or a shortened version of the title:

```
Stimson had been a diplomat and student of
world history and culture for over thirty years
("Stimson").
```

13. Citation of a multivolume work. To cite a page number in a multivolume work that is *not* an alphabetically organized reference work, give the author's name, the volume number, a colon, and the page reference.

```
Truman told the officers and men present that
the bombing was "the greatest thing in history"
(qtd. in Morison 14: 345).
```

14. Citation of more than one page. When citing more than one page, use a hyphen to separate the numbers unless the pages are nonconsecutive:

```
Because of the Quebec Agreement, however,

Roosevelt supported Churchill over Bohr (Rhodes

529-31).
```

When citing consecutive pages, give the complete form of the second number for numbers through 99: 1–2, 13–15, 35–36, 67–69. When citing larger numbers, give only the last two digits of the second number unless more digits are required for clarity's sake: 99–102, 117–18, 223–24, 1201–02, 1201–303.

Preparing the List of Works Cited

Each time you cite a source in your paper, pull the bibliography card for that source from your working bibliography and place it in a new stack of Works Cited cards. When you have completed writing all the parenthetical citations for your paper, you will have a complete set of Works Cited cards. Arrange those cards in alphabetical order. Then type up your final Works Cited list from the cards, following their style exactly. Your final Works Cited list should include a complete bibliographic entry for each source that you have cited in your paper. Here is a sample Works Cited list for a research paper on conservation policies.

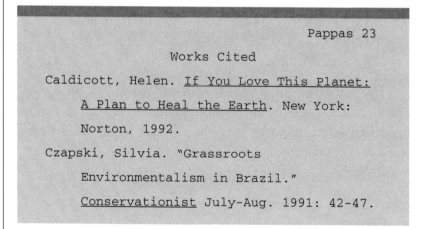

```
                                        Pappas 23
                    Works Cited
Caldicott, Helen. If You Love This Planet:

    A Plan to Heal the Earth. New York:

    Norton, 1992.

Czapski, Silvia. "Grassroots

    Environmentalism in Brazil."

    Conservationist July-Aug. 1991: 42-47.
```

Dietrich, William. <u>The Final Forest: The
    Battle for the Last Great Trees of the
    Pacific Northwest</u>. New York: Simon, 1992.

Frome, Michael. <u>Regreening the National
    Parks</u>. Tucson: U of Arizona P, 1992.

Hamilton, Harriet. "From Stones and Clay
    an Abundance of Trees."
    <u>Conservationist</u> Sep.-Oct. 1991: 32-35.

Harrison, Robert Pogue. <u>Forests: The
    Shadow of Civilization</u>. Chicago: U of
    Chicago P, 1992.

Kahak, E. "Perceiving the Good." <u>The
    Wilderness Condition: Essays on
    Environment and Civilization</u>. Ed. Max
    Oelschaeger. San Francisco: Sierra
    Club, 1992. 173-87.

Kernan, Henry S. "The World Is My Woodlot
    Too." <u>Conservationist</u> Jan.-Feb. 1992:
    44-47.

Ketchledge, Edwin H. "Born-Again Forest."
    <u>Natural History</u> May 1992: 34-38.

Snyder, Gary. "Etiquette of Freedom." <u>The
    Wilderness Condition: Essays on
    Environment and Civilization</u>. Ed. Max
    Oelschaeger. San Francisco: Sierra
    Club, 1992. 21-39.

" Your final Works Cited list should include a complete bibliographic entry for each source that you have cited in your paper. "

If you use more than one work by the same author, alphabetize the works by their titles. Give the author's name for the first work. Thereafter, use three hyphens in place of the name.

```
Steinbeck, John. The Grapes of Wrath.
    1939. New York: Penguin, 1976.
---. Their Blood Is Strong. San Francisco:
    Lubin, 1938. Rpt. in French, Companion
    53-92.
```

If you use several pieces taken from a single work, you can give a complete bibliographic entry for the entire work and cross-reference the entries for the pieces to that entry.

Manuscript Form for the List of Works Cited

1. Begin on a new page.

2. Indent one inch from both side margins.

3. Include your last name and the page number, flush right, half an inch from the top of the paper.

4. Drop down another one-half inch and center the title "Works Cited." Do not underscore it or use all capital letters.

5. Double-space between entries. Double-space between the title and the first entry.

6. Begin each entry at the left margin. Double-space within each entry. Indent run-over lines five spaces from the left margin.

Completing Your Research Paper

After you have finished your documentation, you are ready to proofread your paper and to prepare your final manuscript. **Proofreading** is the process of checking your paper for errors in spelling, grammar, usage, level of language, capitalization, punctuation, and documentation. The **final manuscript** is the copy of your paper that will be read by your teacher and by others.

Proofreading Your Paper

The first step after revising your paper and preparing your documentation is proofreading it to eliminate errors. When you proofread, use symbols like those shown on page 108. The following guidelines are particularly important to keep in mind when you proofread a research paper:

Proofreading a Research Paper

1. Double-check the spellings of proper names, such as the names of people and places.

2. Check to see that the quotations you have used fit grammatically into the sentences in which they appear.

   Ungrammatical: Groves wrote that Szilard did not "evidenced wholehearted cooperation in the maintenance of security."

   Grammatical: Groves wrote that Szilard had not "evidenced wholehearted cooperation in the maintenance of security."

Proofreading a Research Paper (cont.)

3. Check to see that your language is appropriately formal.

4. Check all titles to make sure that these rules have been followed:

   All titles used in the paper should appear in uppercase and lowercase letters. Titles should not be given in all capital letters.

   The following types of words, when appearing in titles, should begin with uppercase letters: adjectives, adverbs, gerunds, interjections, nouns, participles, pronouns, subordinating conjunctions, verbs, words that begin or end the titles, and words that follow colons.

5. Check every sentence to make sure that it has an end mark. If the sentence ends with a parenthetical citation, make sure that the citation appears before the end mark, except in the case of a long, indented quotation, which ends with an end mark followed by the parenthetical citation.

6. Check every quotation in the body of the text to make sure that it begins and ends with quotation marks. Make sure that quotations within quotations in the body of the text are enclosed in single quotation marks. If the quotation is more than four lines long, make sure that it is set off from the body of the text, without quotation marks.

7. Check all titles to make sure that they are punctuated properly.

8. Check to see that points of ellipsis have been used properly in edited quotations. (See page 71.)

Proofreading a Research Paper (cont.)

9. Make sure that every quotation, summary, or paraphrase is followed by a parenthetical citation. Make sure that every citation corresponds to an entry in the Works Cited list.

10. Check every quotation against your note cards to make sure that it is accurate.

Preparing the Final Manuscript

After proofreading, you need to prepare your final manuscript. A recommended manuscript form for research papers is described on the next two pages. You may also wish to refer to the sample research paper on pages 37–51.

After preparing the final manuscript, proofread it one last time. Mark any corrections neatly on the manuscript, using the proofreading symbols shown in the chart on page 108. If a page contains more than three corrections, consider creating a new final page.

Finally, get together all the things that your teacher wishes to see—your paper, including the Works Cited list, and, if requested, your final outline, your note cards, and your bibliography cards. Congratulations! You have just finished your research paper.

Reflecting on the Process

Do some thinking about your experience of writing this paper while it is still fresh in your mind. If you reflect now, you may think of some ways to save yourself time as you work on other research papers. In your journal, write about your research experience. Consider questions such as, What have I learned? What parts of the research process were easiest or most difficult for me? What would I do differently next time?

Guidelines for Manuscript Form: Research Papers

1. **General guidelines/type of paper.** If possible, type or word-process your paper. Use high-quality white, unlined 8½ ″ × 11 ″ paper. Do not use colored paper, transparent paper, onionskin paper, or odd typefaces, such as script. For information on using word-processing programs for research papers, see Appendix A on pages 109–110.

   If you must write your paper out by hand, print or use cursive writing, whichever is neater. Use lined paper, write on only one side of each sheet of paper, and follow the same format guidelines that you would follow when typing or word processing.

2. **Margins.** Use one-inch margins at the top, sides, and bottom.

3. **Name and page numbers.** Include your last name, a space, and the page number at the top of each page of the paper, flush with the right-hand margin. The name and page number should appear one-half inch from the top edge of the paper. Number the pages of the paper and the Works Cited list continuously, using Arabic numerals (1, 2, 3, and so on). Do not precede the page numbers with the word *page* or any abbreviation of it, such as *p.* or *pg.*

4. **Spacing.** Double-space the entire paper, including headings, titles, quotations, and text paragraphs.

5. **Heading.** On the first page, drop down one inch from the top edge of the paper and give, at the left-hand margin and on separate lines, your complete name, your teacher's name, the name of your class, and the complete date in this form: 12 November 1998. Double-space between the lines.

6. **Title.** On the line following the date, center the title of your paper. Use uppercase and lowercase letters, not all capitals, and underline only those words, such as the titles of long works, that you would underline in the body of your paper. Double-space between the date and the title and between the title and the first paragraph of the paper.

Guidelines for Manuscript Form:
Research Papers (cont.)

7. **Indentions.** Indent the first line of each text paragraph five spaces from the left margin.

8. **Quotations.** See the guidelines for quotations on pages 82–83.

9. **Works Cited list.** On the first Works Cited page, after your last name and the page number, drop down an additional one-half inch to a position one inch from the top edge of the paper, and center the title "Works Cited." Do not underline the title or enclose it in quotation marks.

10. **Placement and spacing of Works Cited entries.** Double-space after the title "Works Cited" and begin the first Works Cited entry.

    Double-space and alphabetize all the Works Cited entries. Entries should be alphabetized by their first words, whether the words are parts of titles or of persons' names. If an entry begins with a title, skip any initial article (*a, an,* or *the*) when alphabetizing.

    Begin the first line of each Works Cited entry flush left. Indent subsequent lines five spaces from the left margin.

11. **Binding and presentation.** Do not staple your research paper, and do not use rubber bands. Follow the instructions for binding and presentation given by your teacher. Most teachers will simply ask that you fasten the pages together with a paper clip.

12. **Final outline.** If your teacher asks you to submit a final outline along with your research paper, use one of the formats shown in the sample outlines on pages 77–78. In your final outline, however, your statement of controlling purpose should be replaced with your thesis statement.

Proofreading Symbols

N̸orth of Mexico	Make lowercase.
President jefferson	Capitalize.
a fine ~~thing~~ idea	Replace.
this ~~this~~ time	Delete.
thier	Transpose.
1, 2⌄or 3	Add a comma.
Let⌄s go.	Add an apostrophe.
Welcome, friends⊙	Add a period.
They ⌃ leaving. are	Add letters or words.

Computers and the Research Paper

The widespread availability and use of personal computers has changed the ways in which many people produce research papers. If you have access to a personal computer at home or at school, consider using it to prepare your research paper. The following are some of the ways in which personal computers can be used in the various stages of the research process:

1. **Finding sources.** Many libraries have computerized catalogs that can help you to find sources. You can also use a personal computer to find information directly (see items 2 and 3 below).

2. **Using commercial on-line services.** When you use your computer to communicate with another computer, you are working "on-line." On-line resources include a number of commercial services that are valuable sources of information. These services offer current facts and news; on-line encyclopedias; access to abstracts or full versions of periodical articles, reports, and government documents; homework assistance; tutoring; classes in particular subjects; and research assistance. A few of the on-line services offer connections to institutions such as libraries and museums, including the Library of Congress and the Smithsonian Institution in Washington, D.C. Some services provide access to forums, or ongoing electronic conversations among users interested in particular topics. To subscribe to an on-line service, you need either a computer with a modem linked to a telephone line or a television set with an Internet-ready box. Your school's computer lab or resource center may be linked to a commercial on-line service.

3. **Using the Internet.** The Internet is a vast network of computers used by news services, libraries, universities, researchers, organizations, government agencies, schools, and private individuals. With a computer that is linked to the Internet, you can have access to a huge number of information sources. For example, home pages on the

World Wide Web—one of the Internet's most popular resources—can be a good source of up-to-the-minute information. Your school's computer lab or resource center may be linked to the Internet.

4. **Using CD-ROMs.** If your computer has a CD-ROM drive, you will be able to use some of the many resource materials—from timetables of history and science to encyclopedias to the works of Shakespeare—that are available on CD-ROM. See your local computer dealer about purchasing such discs, or see if your school or community library has a CD-ROM collection.

5. **Preparing computerized bibliography cards and note cards.** If you are familiar with the use of database or hypertext programs, then you know that such programs can easily be used in preparing note cards and bibliography cards. The advantage of preparing note cards and bibliography cards with such programs is that you can sort the entries automatically, in alphabetical or numerical order, according to any element in them, such as the names of authors or editors, the guidelines, or the source numbers.

6. **Using documentation software.** Several programs are now available that generate bibliographies, Works Cited lists, endnotes, and footnotes automatically, and some word-processing programs have built-in documentation features. However, before you use such a program, make sure that it follows the style that is specified in this book—the style described in the *MLA Handbook for Writers of Research Papers.*

7. **Using outlining software.** Many word-processing programs have built-in outlining features. Separate, stand-alone outlining programs are also available. However, be careful that any such program that you use creates outlines in the form described in this book or in a form acceptable to your teacher.

8. **Creating graphics.** Personal computers can, of course, be used to prepare graphics for use in research papers. Excellent programs exist for drawing, for creating charts and tables, for creating graphs of all kinds, and for mapping.

Abbreviations for Use in Research Papers

Dates and Geographical Names

See a dictionary or the *MLA Handbook for Writers of Research Papers* for abbreviations of days, months, and geographical names.

Publishers

When including a publisher's name in a Works Cited entry, footnote, or endnote omit articles (*a, an, the*), abbreviations of business entities (*Co., Inc., Ltd.*), and words that indicate the business that the publisher is in (*Books, House, Press, Publishers*). However, use the abbreviations *U* for "University" and *P* for "Press" in Works Cited entries for university-press publications, as in *MIT P, U of Texas P, U of Puerto Rico P,* and *Cambridge UP.*

Use the following accepted shortened forms of publishers' names. If the publishing-house name consists of a person's name (Jeremy P. Tarcher, Inc.), then use the last name as the shortened form (Tarcher). If the publisher does not appear in the following list or if the name of the publishing house is not a person's name, consult the *MLA Handbook for Writers of Research Papers,* use an abbreviation of your own that clearly identifies the publisher, or give the publisher's name in full, except for the kinds of words described in the preceding paragraph.

Abrams	Harry N. Abrams, Inc.	ALA	American Library Association
Allyn	Allyn and Bacon, Inc.	Appleton	Appleton-Century-Crofts
Ballantine	Ballantine Books, Inc.	Bantam	Bantam Books, Inc.
Barnes	Barnes and Noble Books	Basic	Basic Books
Bobbs	The Bobbs-Merrill Co., Inc.	Clarendon	Clarendon Press

Dell	Dell Publishing Co., Inc.	Dodd	Dodd, Mead and Co.
Doubleday	Doubleday and Co., Inc.	Dover	Dover Publications, Inc.
Dutton	E. P. Dutton, Inc.	Funk	Funk and Wagnalls, Inc.
GPO	Government Printing Office	Harcourt	Harcourt Brace Jovanovich, Inc.
Harper	Harper and Row, Publishers, Inc., or HarperCollins Publishers, Inc.	Holt	Holt, Rinehart, and Winston, Inc.
Houghton	Houghton Mifflin Co.	Knopf	Alfred A. Knopf, Inc.
Lippincott	J. B. Lippincott Co.	Little	Little, Brown and Co.
McDougal	McDougal Littell Inc.	McGraw	McGraw-Hill, Inc.
Macmillan	Macmillan Publishing Co., Inc.	MLA	The Modern Language Association of America
Norton	W. W. Norton and Co., Inc.	Penguin	Penguin Books, Inc.
Pocket	Pocket Books	Prentice	Prentice-Hall, Inc.
Putnam's	G. P. Putnam's Sons	Rand	Rand McNally and Co.
Random	Random House, Inc.	Reader's	Reader's Digest Association
St. Martin's	St. Martin's Press, Inc.	Scott	Scott, Foresman and Co.
Simon	Simon and Schuster, Inc.	Twayne	Twayne Publishers
Viking	The Viking Press, Inc.		

Sacred Works and Literary Works

For abbreviations of parts of the Bible and other scriptures, consult a dictionary. For standard abbreviations of works by Shakespeare and other classic works of literature, see the *MLA Handbook for Writers of Research Papers*.

Other Abbreviations for Use in Documentation

The following abbreviations, in addition to the ones given on the preceding pages, are commonly used in documentation.

abr.	abridged	ch.	chapter
chs.	chapters	col.	column

cols.	columns	comp.	compiled by, compiler
cond.	conducted by, conductor	dir.	directed by, director
ed.	edited by, editor, edition	eds.	editors, editions
et al.	*et alii, et aliae* ("and others")	fig.	figure
fwd.	foreword by, foreword	illus.	illustrated by, illustrator, illustration
introd.	introduced by, introduction	n.d.	no date
no.	number	n.p.	no place, no publisher
P	Press	p.	page
par.	paragraph	pp.	pages
qtd.	quoted	rev.	revised by, revision, review
rpt.	reprinted by, reprint	sc.	scene
sec.	section	ser.	series
trans.	translated by, translator, translation	U	University
vers.	version	vol.	volume
vols.	volumes	writ.	written by, writer

Forms for Working Bibliography and Works Cited Entries

The following are some basic forms for bibliographic entries. Use these forms on the bibliography cards that make up your working bibliography and in the list of works cited that appears at the end of your paper.

Whole Books

The following models can also be used for reports and pamphlets.

A. One author

> Ruiz, Ramón Eduardo. <u>Triumphs and Tragedy: A History of the Mexican People</u>. New York: Norton, 1992.

B. Two authors

> Applewhite, Harriet B., and Darline G. Levy. <u>Women and Politics in the Age of the Democratic Revolution</u>. Ann Arbor: U of Michigan P, 1990.

C. Three authors

> Demko, George J., Jerome Agel, and Eugene Boe. <u>Why in the World: Adventures in Geography</u>. New York: Anchor-Doubleday, 1992.

D. Four or more authors

The abbreviation *et al.* means "and others." Use *et al.* instead of listing all the authors.

> Beringer, Richard E., et al. <u>Why the South Lost the Civil War</u>. Athens: U of Georgia P, 1986.

E. No author given

Literary Market Place: The Directory of the American
      Book Publishing Industry. 1997 ed. New York:
      Bowker, 1996.

F. An editor, but no single author

Nabokov, Peter, ed. Native American Testimony: A
      Chronicle of Indian-White Relations from Prophecy
      to the Present, 1492-1992. New York: Viking-
      Penguin, 1991.

G. Two or three editors

Harrison, Maureen, and Steve Gilbert, eds. Landmark
      Decisions of the United States Supreme Court.
      Beverly Hills: Excellent, 1991.

H. Four or more editors

The abbreviation *et al.* means "and others." Use *et al.* instead of listing all the editors.

McFarlan, Donald, et al., eds. The Guinness Book of
      Records 1992. New York: Facts on File, 1991.

I. An author and a translator

Levi, Primo. Survival in Auschwitz: The Nazi Assault on
      Humanity. Trans. Stuart Woolf. New York: Collier-
      Macmillan, 1987.

J. An author, a translator, and an editor

Capellanus, Andreas. The Art of Courtly Love. Abr. ed.
      Trans. John J. Parry. Ed. Frederick W. Locke. New
      York: Ungar, 1976.

K. An edition other than the first

Janson, H. W., and Anthony F. Janson. History of Art
      for Young People. 4th ed. New York: Abrams, 1992.

L. A book or monograph that is part of a series

```
LaRusso, Carol Spenard, comp. The Green Thoreau.
    Classic Wisdom Ser. San Rafael: New World
    Library, 1992.
```

M. A multivolume work

If you have used only one volume of a multivolume work, cite only that volume.

```
Kimball, Warren F., ed. Churchill and Roosevelt: The
    Complete Correspondence. Vol. 3. Princeton:
    Princeton UP, 1984. 3 vols.
```

If you have used more than one volume of a multivolume work, cite the entire work.

```
Kimball, Warren F., ed. Churchill and Roosevelt: The
    Complete Correspondence. 3 vols. Princeton:
    Princeton UP, 1984.
```

N. A volume with its own title that is part of a multivolume work with a different title

```
Durant, Will, and Ariel Durant. Rousseau and
    Revolution: A History of Civilization in France,
    England, and Germany from 1756, and in the
    Remainder of Europe from 1715, to 1789. New York:
    Simon, 1967. Vol. 10 of The Story of Civilization.
    11 vols. 1935-75.
```

O. A republished book or a literary work available in several editions

Give the date of the original publication after the title. Then give complete publication information, including the date, for the edition that you have used.

```
Steinbeck, John. The Grapes of Wrath. 1939. New York:
    Penguin, 1976.
```

P. A government publication

Give the name of the government (country or state). Then give the department if applicable, followed by the agency if applicable. Next give the title, followed by the author if known. Then give the publication information. The publisher of U.S. government documents is usually the Government Printing Office, or GPO.

United States. Dept. of Education. Office of Educational
    Research and Improvement. <u>OERI Publications Guide</u>.
    By Lance Ferderer. Washington: GPO, 1990.

---. ---. ---. Educational Resources Information
    Center. <u>Recent Department of Education
    Publications in ERIC</u>. Washington: GPO, 1992.

Parts of Books

A. A poem, short story, essay, or chapter in a collection of works by one author

Cather, Willa. "Joseph and His Brothers." <u>Cather:
    Stories, Poems, and Other Writings</u>. Comp. Sharon
    O'Brien. New York: Viking, 1992. 859-71.

B. A poem, short story, essay, or chapter in a collection of works by several authors

West, Paul. "Pelé." <u>The Norton Book of Sports</u>. Ed.
    George Plimpton. New York: Norton, 1992. 308.

C. A novel or play in an anthology

Simmons, Alexander. <u>Sherlock Holmes and the Hands of
    Othello</u>. <u>Black Thunder: An Anthology of
    Contemporary African American Drama</u>. Ed. William
    B. Branch. New York: Mentor, 1992. 359-415.

D. An introduction, preface, foreword, or afterword written by the author(s) of a work

Pinson, Linda, and Jerry Jinnett. Dedication. <u>The Woman
    Entrepreneur</u>. Ed. Pinson and Jinnett. Tustin: Out
    of Your Mind, 1992. [iii]

E. An introduction, preface, foreword, or afterword written by someone other than the author(s) of a work

```
Coles, Robert. Foreword. No Place to Be: Voices of
     Homeless Children. By Judith Berck. Boston:
     Houghton, 1992. 1-4.
```

F. Cross-references

If you have used more than one work from a collection, you may give a complete entry for the collection. Then, in the separate entries for the works, you can refer to the entry for the whole collection by using the editor's last name or, if you have listed more than one work by that editor, the editor's last name and a shortened version of the title.

```
French, Warren, ed. A Companion to The Grapes of Wrath.
     New York:Viking, 1963.

---. "What Did John Steinbeck Know About the 'Okies'?"
     French, Companion 51-53.

Steinbeck, John. Their Blood Is Strong. San Francisco:
     Lubin, 1938. Rpt. in French, Companion 53-92.
```

G. A reprinted article or essay (one previously published elsewhere)

If a work that appears in a collection first appeared in another place, give complete information for the original publication, followed by *Rpt. in* and complete information for the collection.

```
Meier, August. "Toward a Reinterpretation of Booker T.
     Washington." Journal of Southern History 23
     (1957): 220-27. Rpt. in The Making of Black
     America: Essays in Negro Life and History. Ed.
     August Meier and Elliott Rudwick. Vol. 2. New
     York: Atheneum, 1969. 125-30.
```

Magazines, Journals, Newspapers, and Encyclopedias

A. An article in a magazine, journal, or newspaper

Smith, Shelley. "Baseball's Forgotten Pioneers." <u>Sports</u>
    <u>Illustrated</u> 30 Mar. 1992: 72.

Schwartz, Felice N. "Women as a Business Imperative."
    <u>Harvard Business Review</u> 70.2 (1992): 105-13.

"Kozyrev's Mission to Washington." Editorial. <u>Boston</u>
    <u>Globe</u> 14 June 1992: 78.

If no author is given, begin with the article's title. If an author is given, begin with the author's name followed by the article's title. When an article continues on a different, nonconsecutive page, use a plus sign (+) after the number of the page on which it begins.

B. An article in an encyclopedia or other alphabetically organized reference work

Give the title of the article, the name of the reference work, and the year of the edition.

"Zuni." <u>Encyclopaedia Britannica: Micropaedia</u>. 1992 ed.

C. A review

Gutiérrez, David G. Rev. of <u>Conquests and Historical</u>
    <u>Identities in California, 1769-1936</u>, by Lisbeth
    Haas. <u>American Historical Review</u> 101.5 (1996):
    1610-11.

If the review is unsigned, begin with *Rev. of* and the title.

Media and Other Sources

A. An interview you have conducted or letter you have received

```
Jackson, Jesse. Personal interview [or Letter to the
    author]. 15 July 1992.
```

B. A film

```
Glory. Screenplay by Kevin Jarre. Dir. Edward Zwick.
    Perf. Matthew Broderick, Morgan Freeman, and Denzel
    Washington. TriStar, 1989.
```

C. A work of art

```
Catlin, George. Four Bears, Second Chief, in Full
    Dress. National Museum of American Art,
    Smithsonian Institution, Washington.
```

D. A television program

Give the episode name (if applicable) and the series or program name. Include any information that you have about the program's writer and director. Then give the network, the local station, the city, and the date the program aired.

```
"A Desert Blooming." Writ. Marshall Riggan. Living
    Wild. Dir. Harry L. Gorden. PBS. WTTW, Chicago.
    29 Apr. 1984.
```

E. A musical composition

```
Chopin, Frédéric. Waltz in A-flat major, op. 42.
```

F. A recording (compact disc, LP, or audiocassette)

If the recording is not a compact disc, include *LP* or *Audiocassette* before the manufacturer's name.

```
Guthrie, Woody. "Do-Re-Me." Dust Bowl Ballads.
    Rounder, 1988.
```

G. A lecture, speech, or address

Give the name of the speaker followed by the name of the speech, if available, or the kind of speech (*Lecture, Introduction, Address*). Then give the event, the place, and the date.

```
Benjamin, John. Address. First Annual Abolitionist
     March and Rally. Boston, 18 July 1992.
```

Electronic Media

Because the number of electronic information sources is great and increasing rapidly, please refer to the most current edition of the MLA Handbook for Writers of Research Papers *if you need more complete information.*

Portable databases (CD-ROMs, videodiscs, diskettes, and videocassettes)

These products contain fixed information (information that cannot be changed unless a new version is produced and released). Citing them in a research paper is similar to citing printed sources. You should include the following:

- Name of the author, if applicable
- Title of the part of the work, if applicable (underlined or in quotation marks)
- Title of the product or database (underlined)
- Edition, release, or version, if applicable
- Publication medium (CD-ROM, videodisc, diskette, or videocassette)
- City of publication
- Name of the publisher
- Year of publication

If you cannot find some of this information, cite what is available.

```
Boyer, Paul S., et al. "Troubled Agriculture." The
     Enduring Vision: A History of the American People,
     Interactive Edition. Vers. 1.1. CD-ROM. Lexington:
     Heath, 1993.

"Steinbeck's Dust Bowl Saga." Our Times Multimedia
     Encyclopedia of the 20th Century. 1996 ed. CD-ROM.
     Redwood City: Vicarious, 1995.

"The Cold War Comes Home: Hollywood Blacklists the Kahn
     Family." American Stories: Videodisc. Evanston:
     McDougal, 1998.

Eyes on the Prize: America's Civil Rights Years. Prod.
     Blackside. Videocassette. PBS Video, 1986.
```

On-line databases

Because on-line databases may be updated or changed frequently, it is important to include complete information when citing them:

- Name of the author, if applicable
- Title of the material accessed (in quotation marks)
- Date of the material, if applicable
- Title of the database (underlined)
- Publication medium (*Online*)
- Name of the computer service or computer network (e.g., *Prodigy, Internet*)
- Date of access (the date you found the information on-line)

> "Drought." <u>Compton's Living Encyclopedia</u>. Online.
> America Online. 18 May 1997.

> "Nebraska data." <u>1990 Census Lookup</u>. Online. Internet.
> 8 Jan. 1997.

> "Great North American Prairie Ecoregion." <u>Sierra Club
> Foundation</u>. Online. Internet. 19 Dec. 1996.

Electronic texts of many literary works and historical documents are available on-line. You should be aware that not all texts are equally reliable. Try to use a text that gives the title, editor, and date of publication of the work. Include the following in your citation:

- Name of the author, if applicable
- Title of the text (underlined)
- Publication information for the printed source
- Publication medium (*Online*)
- Name of the repository of the electronic text (e.g., *Oxford Text Archive*)
- Name of the computer network
- Date of access (the date you found the information on-line)

> Dickens, Charles. <u>A Christmas Carol</u>. London: Chapman,
> 1893. Online. Oxford Text Archive. Internet. 19
> Sep. 1997.

> Whitman, Walt. <u>Leaves of Grass</u>. Philadelphia: McKay,
> 1900. Online. Columbia U Academic Information
> Systems. Internet. 8 Mar. 1998.

Alternative Documentation Styles

The documentation style suggested in this book, which involves parenthetical citations and a list of works cited, is recommended in the *MLA Handbook for Writers of Research Papers* and is widely used for work in language, literature, the arts, and the humanities throughout the English-speaking world. However, other approaches to documentation are possible. One common approach is to use endnotes or footnotes in place of parenthetical citations.

Endnote and Footnote Style

Some people prefer endnotes or footnotes because they remove the clutter of citations from the text of the research paper. Instead of a citation, what appears in the text is a number placed after a sentence and above the line, as in the following example:

```
Colonel Shaw's mother is said to have cried from

happiness on seeing her son at the head of the all-

African-American 54th Massachusetts.5
```

The number that is placed above the line is called a **superscript.** Throughout the paper, each instance of material taken from a source is marked with such a superscript. The superscript refers the reader to a note that appears either at the bottom of the page on which the superscript appears or at the end of the paper. If the note appears at the bottom of the page, it is called a **footnote.** If it appears at the end of the paper, it is called an **endnote.** Footnotes have become unpopular in recent years because of their tendency to clutter the pages of a paper. Most writers who use notes instead of parenthetical citations prefer endnotes. The following is a sample endnote or footnote:

```
     5 Shelby Foote, Fredericksburg to Meridian (New York:

Random, 1963), vol. 2 of The Civil War: A Narrative, 3

vols. (1958-74) 697.
```

An endnote or footnote differs from a working bibliography or Works Cited entry in the following ways:

1. The first line of a working bibliography or Works Cited entry begins at the left margin. The first line of an endnote or footnote is indented five spaces.

2. Run-over lines of a working bibliography or Works Cited entry are indented five spaces. Run-over lines of an endnote or footnote begin at the left margin.

3. A working bibliography or Works Cited entry does not have a superscript at the beginning. An endnote or footnote does.

4. The name at the beginning of a working bibliography or Works Cited entry is reversed for alphabetizing. In an endnote or footnote, the name is given in its normal order.

5. A working bibliography or Works Cited entry has three main parts, each of which ends with a period: the name, the title, and the publication information. An endnote or footnote has four main parts, only the last of which ends with a period: the name, the title, the publication information, and the page number(s).

6. The publication information in an endnote or footnote is enclosed in parentheses, whereas in a working bibliography or Works Cited entry it is not.

For proper placement of endnotes and footnotes, see the samples on pages 141–143. The table on the following pages gives sample forms for endnotes and footnotes.

Sample Entries for Endnotes and Footnotes

Whole Books

The following models can also be used for reports and pamphlets.

A. One author

¹ Ramón Eduardo Ruiz, <u>Triumphs and Tragedy: A History of the Mexican People</u> (New York: Norton, 1992) 14.

B. Two authors

² Harriet B. Applewhite and Darline G. Levy, <u>Women and Politics in the Age of the Democratic Revolution</u> (Ann Arbor: U of Michigan P, 1990) 63.

C. Three authors

³ George J. Demko, Jerome Agel, and Eugene Boe, <u>Why in the World: Adventures in Geography</u> (New York: Anchor-Doubleday, 1992) 15-16.

D. Four or more authors

The abbreviation *et al.* means "and others." Use *et al.* instead of listing all the authors.

⁴ Richard E. Beringer et al., <u>Why the South Lost the Civil War</u> (Athens: U of Georgia P, 1986) 56.

E. No author given

⁵ <u>Literary Market Place: The Directory of the American Book Publishing Industry</u>, 1997 ed. (New York: Bowker, 1996) 1673.

F. An editor, but no single author

⁶ Peter Nabokov, ed., <u>Native American Testimony: A Chronicle of Indian-White Relations from Prophecy to the Present, 1492-1992</u> (New York: Viking-Penguin, 1991) 101.

G. Two or three editors

⁷ Maureen Harrison and Steve Gilbert, eds., <u>Landmark</u>

<u>Decisions of the United States Supreme Court</u> (Beverly Hills: Excellent, 1991) 106.

H. Four or more editors

The abbreviation *et al.* means "and others." Use *et al.* instead of listing all the editors.

    [8] Donald McFarlan et al., eds., <u>The Guinness Book of Records 1992</u> (New York: Facts on File, 1991) 99.

I. An author and a translator

    [9] Primo Levi, <u>Survival in Auschwitz: The Nazi Assault on Humanity</u>, trans. Stuart Woolf (New York: Collier-Macmillan, 1987) 115.

J. An author, a translator, and an editor

    [10] Andreas Capellanus, <u>The Art of Courtly Love</u>, abr. ed., trans. John J. Parry, ed. Frederick W. Locke (New York: Ungar, 1976) 42.

K. An edition other than the first

    [11] H. W. Janson and Anthony F. Janson, <u>History of Art for Young People</u>, 4th ed. (New York: Abrams, 1992) 45.

L. A book or monograph that is part of a series

    [12] Carol Spenard LaRusso, comp., <u>The Green Thoreau</u>, Classic Wisdom Ser. (San Rafael: New World Library, 1992) 47.

M. A multivolume work

If you are referring to a particular place in one volume, use this form:

    [13] Warren F. Kimball, ed., <u>Churchill and Roosevelt: The Complete Correspondence</u>, vol. 3 (Princeton: Princeton UP, 1984) 228.

Endnotes and footnotes that refer to entire works are quite rare. However, if you are referring to an entire multivolume work, use the following form, with no page number:

    [14] Warren F. Kimball, ed., <u>Churchill and Roosevelt: The Complete Correspondence</u>, 3 vols. (Princeton: Princeton UP, 1984)

N. A volume with its own title that is part of a multivolume work with a different title

15 Will Durant and Ariel Durant, <u>Rousseau and Revolution: A History of Civilization in France, England, and Germany from 1756, and in the Remainder of Europe from 1715, to 1789</u> (New York: Simon, 1967), vol. 10 of <u>The Story of Civilization</u>, 11 vols. (1935-75) 18.

O. A republished book or a literary work available in several editions

Give the date of the original publication, followed by a semicolon, before the complete publication information for the edition that you have used.

16 John Steinbeck, <u>The Grapes of Wrath</u> (1939; New York: Penguin, 1989) 339.

P. A government publication

Give the name of the government (country or state). Then give the department, if applicable, followed by the agency, if applicable. Next give the title, followed by the author, if known. Then give the publication information. The publisher of U.S. government documents is usually the Government Printing Office, or GPO.

17 United States, Dept. of Education, Office of Educational Research and Improvement, <u>OERI Publications Guide</u>, by Lance Ferderer (Washington: GPO, 1990) 27.

18 ---, ---, ---, Educational Resources Information Center, <u>Recent Department of Education Publications in ERIC</u> (Washington: GPO, 1992) 162.

Parts of Books

A. A poem, short story, essay, or chapter in a collection of works by one author

19 Willa Cather, "Joseph and His Brothers," <u>Cather: Stories, Poems, and Other Writings</u>, comp. Sharon O'Brien (New York: Viking, 1992) 860.

B. A poem, short story, essay, or chapter in a collection of works by several authors

[20] Paul West, "Pelé," <u>The Norton Book of Sports</u>, ed. George Plimpton (New York: Norton, 1992) 308.

C. A novel or play in an anthology

[21] Alexander Simmons, <u>Sherlock Holmes and the Hands of Othello</u>, <u>Black Thunder: An Anthology of Contemporary African American Drama</u>, ed. William B. Branch (New York: Mentor, 1992) 411.

D. An introduction, preface, foreword, or afterword written by the author(s) of a work

[22] Linda Pinson and Jerry Jinnett, dedication, <u>The Woman Entrepreneur</u>, ed. Pinson and Jinnett (Tustin: Out of Your Mind, 1992) [iii]

E. An introduction, preface, foreword, or afterword written by someone other than the author(s) of a work

[23] Robert Coles, foreword, <u>No Place to Be: Voices of Homeless Children</u>, by Judith Berck (Boston: Houghton, 1992) 2.

F. A reprinted article or essay (one previously published elsewhere)

If a work that appears in a collection first appeared in another place, give complete information for the original publication, followed by *rpt. in* and complete information for the collection.

[24] August Meier, "Toward a Reinterpretation of Booker T. Washington," <u>Journal of Southern History</u> 23 (1957): 220-27, rpt. in <u>The Making of Black America: Essays in Negro Life and History</u>, ed. August Meier and Elliot Rudwick, vol. 2 (New York: Atheneum, 1969) 125-30.

Magazines, Journals, Newspapers, and Encyclopedias

A. An article in a magazine, journal, or newspaper

[25] Shelley Smith, "Baseball's Forgotten Pioneers," <u>Sports Illustrated</u> 30 Mar. 1992: 72.

26 Felice N. Schwartz, "Women as a Business Imperative," <u>Harvard Business Review</u> 70.2 (1992): 105-13.

27 "Kozyrev's Mission to Washington," editorial, <u>Boston Globe</u> 14 June 1992: 78.

If no author is given, begin with the article's title. If an author is given, begin with the author's name followed by the article's title. When referring to an entire article printed on nonconsecutive pages, use a plus sign (+) after the number of the page on which it begins.

B. An article in an encyclopedia or other alphabetically organized reference work

Give the title of the article, the name of the reference work, and the year of the edition.

28 "Zuni," <u>Encyclopaedia Britannica: Micropaedia</u>, 1992 ed.

C. A review

29 David G. Gutiérrez, rev. of <u>Conquests and Historical Identities in California, 1769-1936</u>, by Lisbeth Haas, <u>American Historical Review</u> 101.5 (1996): 1610-11.

Media and Other Sources

A. An interview you have conducted or letter you have received

30 Jesse Jackson, personal interview [*or* letter to the author], 15 July 1992.

B. A film

31 <u>Glory</u>, screenplay by Kevin Jarre, dir. Edward Zwick, perf. Matthew Broderick, Morgan Freeman, and Denzel Washington, TriStar, 1989.

C. A work of art

32 George Catlin, <u>Four Bears, Second Chief, in Full Dress</u>, National Museum of American Art, Smithsonian Institution, Washington.

D. A television program

Give the episode name (if applicable) and the series or program name. Include any information that you have about the program's writer and director. Then give the network, the local station, the city, and the date the program aired.

[33] "A Desert Blooming," writ. Marshall Riggan, <u>Living Wild</u>, dir. Harry L. Gorden, PBS, WTTW, Chicago, 29 Apr. 1984.

E. A musical composition

[34] Frédéric Chopin, Waltz in A-flat major, op. 42.

F. A recording (compact disc, LP, or audiocassette)

If the recording is not a compact disc, include *LP* or *audiocassette* before the manufacturer's name.

[35] Woody Guthrie, "Do-Re-Me," <u>Dust Bowl Ballads</u>, Rounder, 1988.

G. A lecture, speech or address

Give the name of the speaker followed by the name of the speech, if available, or the kind of speech (*lecture, introduction, address*). Then give the event, the place, and the date.

[36] John Benjamin, address, First Annual Abolitionist March and Rally, Boston, 18 July 1992.

Electronic Media

Because the number of electronic information sources is great and increasing rapidly, please refer to the most current edition of the MLA Handbook for Writers of Research Papers *if you need more complete information.*

Portable databases (CD-ROM, videodiscs, diskettes, and videocassettes)

These products contain fixed information (information that cannot be changed unless a new version is produced and released). Citing them in a research paper is similar to citing printed sources. You should include the following:

- Name of the author, if applicable
- Title of the part of the work, if applicable (underlined or in quotation marks)
- Title of the product or database (underlined)
- Edition, release, or version, if applicable
- Publication medium (CD-ROM, videodisc, diskette, or videocassette)
- City of publication
- Name of the publisher
- Year of publication

If you cannot find some of this information, cite what is available.

37 Paul S. Boyer et al., "Troubled Agriculture," The Enduring Vision: A History of the American People, Interactive Edition, vers. 1.1, CD-ROM (Lexington: Heath, 1993).

38 "Steinbeck's Dust Bowl Saga," Our Times Multimedia Encyclopedia of the 20th Century, 1996 ed., CD-ROM (Redwood City: Vicarious, 1995).

39 "The Cold War Comes Home: Hollywood Blacklists the Kahn Family," American Stories, videodisc (Evanston: McDougal, 1998).

40 Eyes on the Prize: America's Civil Rights Years, prod. Blackside, videocassette, PBS Video, 1986.

On-line databases

Because on-line databases may be updated or changed frequently, it is important to include complete information when citing them:

- Name of the author, if applicable
- Title of the material accessed (in quotation marks)
- Date of the material, if applicable
- Title of the database (underlined)
- Publication medium (*online*)
- Name of the computer service or computer network (e.g., *CompuServe, America Online, Prodigy, Internet*)
- Date of access (the date you found the information on-line)

41 "Drought," <u>Compton's Living Encyclopedia</u>, online, America Online, 18 May 1997.

42 "Nebraska data," <u>1990 Census Lookup</u>, online, Internet, 8 Jan. 1997.

43 "Great North American Prairie Ecoregion," <u>Sierra Club Foundation</u>, online, Internet, 19 Dec. 1996.

Electronic texts of many literary works and historical documents are available on-line (often through universities and government agencies). You should be aware that not all texts are equally reliable. Try to use a text that gives the title, editor, and date of publication of the work. Check with a librarian or your teacher if you have questions about the reliability of on-line sources. You should include the following:

- Name of the author, if applicable
- Title of the text (underlined)
- Publication information for the printed source
- Publication medium (*online*)
- Name of the repository of the electronic text (e.g., *Oxford Text Archive*)
- Name of the computer network
- Date of access (the date you found the information on-line)

44 Charles Dickens, <u>A Christmas Carol</u> (London: Chapman, 1893), online, Oxford Text Archive, Internet, 19 Sep. 1997.

45 Walt Whitman, <u>Leaves of Grass</u> (Philadelphia: McKay, 1900), online, Columbia U Academic Information Systems, Internet, 8 Mar. 1998.

Subsequent References

The first time that you write an endnote or footnote for a work, give a full entry. Thereafter, you can give the author's or editor's name by itself:

51 Warren French, "What Did John Steinbeck Know About the 'Okies'?" <u>A Companion to</u> The Grapes of Wrath, ed. French (New York: Viking, 1963) 52.

⁵² French 53.

If you have cited more than one work by the author or editor, then include shortened forms of the titles in subsequent endnotes or footnotes:

⁵³ French, "What Did" 53.

Other Types of Documentation

Two other documentation styles are in widespread use today. The **author-date** system is widely used in the sciences. This system is similar to parenthetical documentation, but each parenthetical citation includes, after the author's or editor's last name, the date of publication.

    Wendell Phillips, a leader of the Boston abolition-

    ists, had declared, "We have given the sword to the

    white man; the time has come to give it to the

    black!" (Burchard, 1965, 43).

As the following examples show, the Works Cited entries used in the author-date system differ in a number of ways, from those used in the parenthetical-documentation system. For details about the preparation of such entries, see the *Publication Manual of the American Psychological Association.*

    Burchard, P. (1965). <u>One gallant rush: Robert Gould</u>

    <u>Shaw and his brave black regiment</u>. New York: St. Martin's

    Press.

    Foote, S. (1958-74). <u>The Civil War: A narrative</u>. (Vols.

    1-3). New York: Random House.

```
Schwartz, F. N. (1992). Women as a business imperative.
```

Harvard Business Review, 70 (2), 105-13.

In the **number system** of documentation, each entry in the Works Cited list
is numbered with an Arabic numeral (1, 2, 3, and so on). The entries are
usually arranged in the order in which the works are cited in the research
paper. Here are two examples of such entries:

1. Burchard, P. One gallant rush: Robert Gould Shaw and

    his brave black regiment. New York: St. Martin's Press,

    1965.

2. Foote, S. The Civil War: A narrative. New York: Random

    House, 1958-74.

A parenthetical citation in the text of the research paper consists of the number of a Works Cited entry, a comma, the abbreviation *p.* or *pp.*, and the
relevant page number(s).

Wendell Phillips, a leader of the Boston abolition-

ists, had declared, "We have given the sword to the

white man; the time has come to give it to the

black!" (1, p. 43).

Other Style Manuals

The documentation style used in this book is that of the *MLA Handbook for Writers of Research Papers.* Other style manuals that are widely used, especially in social studies and the humanities, are the following:

The Chicago Manual of Style

A Manual for Writers of Term Papers, Theses, and Dissertations, by Kate Turabian

Publication Manual of the American Psychological Association

Marcus Washington

Mr. Zacharis

American History

3 May 1998

This is a sample paper done in endnote style. For a sample done in footnote style, see page 143.

                    The "Victory" of the Massachusetts 54th

                              at Fort Wagner

        On Boston Common, near the Massachusetts State House,
stands an impressive monument--a sculpture depicting a group
of African-American soldiers marching in the uniforms of the
Union Army.[1] This monument commemorates the brave men of the
Massachusetts 54th Infantry Regiment, who on July 18, 1863, at
the height of the Civil War, stormed a South Carolina
earthwork known as Fort Wagner or Battery Wagner. When the
fighting was done, nearly half of those men lay dead in what
was by all accounts a massacre, an overwhelming victory for
the Confederacy.[2] However, the events at Fort Wagner were
strangely contradictory. Although many Yankee soldiers lost
their lives in the charge, and although the Confederates
technically won the battle, one can rightly claim that the
battle was a great victory for the Union Army and for all
people of color.

        The first calls for recruitment of African-American
soldiers into the Union Army came from abolitionist leaders.
Frederick Douglass, the charismatic African-American orator,
newspaper editor, and abolitionist, had proclaimed, "The arm
of the slaves [is] the best defense against the arm of the
slaveholder. . . . Who would be free themselves must strike
the blow."[3] Wendell Phillips, a leader of the Boston
abolitionists, had declared, "We have given the sword to the
white man; the time has come to give it to the black!"[4]
According to historian Barbara Fields, a convention of free
African Americans meeting in 1863 resolved: "It is time now

Note that numbers referring to endnotes are **superscripted**, or raised above the line.

The brackets enclose a slight modification made to the source in order to fit it grammatically into the paper.

for more effective remedies to be thoroughly tried in the
shape of warm lead and cold steel duly administered by 100,000
black doctors."[5] By that time, Congress had authorized the
enlistment of African-American troops, a move that met with
the full support of Ulysses S. Grant:

> I have given the subject of arming the Negro my
> hearty support. This, with the emancipation of the
> Negro, is the heaviest blow yet given the
> Confederacy. . . . [W]e have added a powerful ally.
> They will make good soldiers and taking them from
> the enemy weakens him in the same proportion they
> strengthen us.[6]

The African-American 54th Massachusetts Infantry Regiment
was the brainchild of Governor John A. Andrew, who on January
26, 1863, had responded to Lincoln's Emancipation Proclamation
by writing to Edwin Stanton, Lincoln's secretary of war,
requesting permission to raise a regiment of troops of
African-American descent.[7] To lead the regiment, Andrew chose
a young soldier named Robert Gould Shaw, from a staunchly
antislavery family in Boston.[8] By May 14, one thousand men
had volunteered to serve in the 54th.[9] For some time,
however, the Union commanders were reluctant to put their
African-American troops into combat.[10] On July 6, Colonel
Shaw wrote to Brigadier General George C. Strong, complaining
that his men were not being put to use.[11] On July 18, Shaw
and his regiment got their chance to see action.

Fort Wagner, "perhaps the strongest [earthwork] ever
built," sat on the Atlantic coast at the mouth of Charleston
Harbor. Taking Fort Wagner was part of the Union Army's
overall plan to take the city of Charleston.[12] Unfortunately
for the Union troops, the only approach to the fort was a
narrow area less than two hundred yards wide.[13] Any troops

Note that a superscript
is placed outside a
final quotation mark.

A long quotation is set
off from the text and
indented ten spaces.
The superscript is
placed at the end of
the quotation.

crossing that area would be in grave danger from the Confederate troops stationed inside the fort. Colonel Shaw enthusiastically agreed to lead the attack on Fort Wagner.[14] The attack began at 7:30 at night:

> The 1000-man rebel garrison came out of the bombproof to which it had retired at the height of the cannonade and met the attackers. . . . When flesh and blood could stand no more, the survivors fell back from the ditch and parapet, black and white alike, and returned to the trenches they had left an hour ago. Casualties had been heavy; 1515 of the attackers had fallen, as compared to 174 of the defenders. . . . [N]ext morning . . . a brief truce sufficed for removal of the wounded and disposal of the slain, including the twenty-six-year-old Shaw.[15]

It was a terrible defeat, and yet there are two reasons for considering it a victory as well. The first reason is that the charge helped to create an attitude both within the men of the 54th and within many whites that would make it difficult for any Americans of African descent to be made slaves again. The second reason is that the charge proved the value of African-American soldiers and led to their further participation in the war.

The bravery of the 54th Massachusetts proved that African Americans could be good soldiers. After the charge on Fort Wagner, the numbers of African-American enlisted men grew. A total of 180,000 African-American soldiers served with the Union Army during the last years of the war--a force equal to an astonishing 85 percent of the eligible male African-American population.[16]

The charge on Fort Wagner was also a powerful blow against slavery. The institution of slavery depended on the ability of people to believe that some human beings were inherently less capable or less worthy than others. As Confederate general Howell Cobb had put it, "If slaves seem good soldiers, then our whole theory of slavery is wrong."[17] The men of the 54th were determined to prove that the theory was wrong. As one member of the 54th is reported to have said, "We want 'em to know that we went down standing up."[18] By not flinching from their duty, by charging onward against overwhelming odds, the men of the 54th demonstrated their courage and the falsehood of the racist assumption of lesser worth underlying slavery. General William Tecumseh Sherman of the Union forces pointed out, after African-American soldiers took up arms, "They [the South] can't get back their slaves. It is dead."[19] It was the fulfillment of a prophecy that Frederick Douglass had made:

> Once let a black man get upon his person the brass letters, "U.S." . . . [l]et him get an eagle on his buttons and a musket on his shoulder and bullets in his pocket, and there is no power on earth which can deny that he has earned the right to citizenship in the United States.[20]

The charge of the 54th is considered by many African Americans today a critical point in history, a point when their ancestors established their right to citizenship. Monica Fairbanks, director of the Afro-American History Museum in Boston, quotes with approval William Carney, a member of the Massachusetts 54th who was awarded the Congressional Medal of Honor: "We . . . take up arms in defense of a nation to which we belong."[21] State Senator Bill Orin of Massachusetts considers celebration of the memory of the Massachusetts 54th to be equivalent to "celebrating the diversity of the United States of America."[22] John Benjamin of the National Park Service speaks of the importance of having the world recognize "the contribution of the 54th to the freedom of our people."[23] Gloria Fox, a Massachusetts state representative, says, "The struggle continues—that's what [remembering] the 54th means."[24] Each of these leaders recognizes the charge of the 54th not as a defeat but as a great moral victory—a victory pulled, as the proverb has it, "from the jaws of defeat." That the charge of the Massachusetts 54th is today remembered in this way is a fulfillment of a prediction made by Abraham Lincoln:

> When victory is won, there will be some black men who can remember that, with silent tongue and clenched teeth and steady eye and well-poised bayonet, they have helped mankind on to a great consummation.[25]

Ending with a quotation is one innovative way to conclude a research paper or report.

Notes

1 Augustus Saint-Gaudens, <u>Monument to Robert Gould Shaw and His Regiment</u>, Boston Common, Boston.

2 Geoffrey Ward, <u>The Civil War: An Illustrated History</u> (New York: Knopf, 1990) 248.

3 "The Universe of Battle," <u>The Civil War</u>, dir. Ken Burns, videocassette, PBS Video, 1990.

4 Peter Burchard, <u>One Gallant Rush: Robert Gould Shaw and His Brave Black Regiment</u> (New York: St. Martin's, 1965) 43.

5 Ward 246-47.

6 Ward 247.

7 Burchard 2.

8 Burchard 71.

9 Burchard 90.

10 Ward 247.

11 Burchard 117-18.

12 Burchard 120-21.

13 Shelby Foote, <u>Fredericksburg to Meridian</u> (New York: Random, 1963), vol. 2 of <u>The Civil War: A Narrative</u>, 3 vols. (1958-74) 697.

14 Burchard 133.

15 Foote 697.

16 "Universe."

17 Qtd. in Ward 253.

18 <u>Glory</u>, Screenplay by Kevin Jarre, dir. Edward Zwick, perf. Matthew Broderick, Morgan Freeman, and Denzel Washington, TriStar, 1989.

19 Qtd. in "Universe."

20 Qtd. in Ward 246.

21 Monica Fairbanks, personal interview, 18 July 1992.

22 Bill Orin, address, First Annual Abolitionist March and Rally, Boston, 18 July 1992.

[23] John Benjamin, address, First Annual Abolitionist March and Rally, Boston, 18 July 1992.

[24] Gloria Fox, greetings, Abolitionist Rally at the African Meeting House, Boston, 18 July 1992.

[25] Qtd. in "Universe."

Marcus Washington

Mr. Zacharis

American History

3 May 1998

The Victory of the Massachusetts 54th

at Fort Wagner

On Boston Common, near the Massachusetts State House, stands an impressive monument--a sculpture depicting a group of African-American soldiers marching in the uniforms of the Union Army.[1] This monument commemorates the brave men of the Massachusetts 54th Infantry Regiment, who on July 18, 1863, at the height of the Civil War, stormed a South Carolina earthwork known as Fort Wagner or Battery Wagner. When the fighting was done, nearly half of those men lay dead in what was by all accounts a massacre, an overwhelming victory for the Confederacy.[2] However, the events at Fort Wagner were strangely contradictory. Although many Yankee soldiers lost their lives in the charge, and although the Confederates technically won the battle, one can rightly claim that the battle was a great victory for the Union Army and for all people of color.

The first calls for recruitment of African-American soldiers into the Union Army came from abolitionist leaders. Frederick Douglass, the charismatic African-American orator, newspaper editor, and abolitionist, had proclaimed, "The arm of the slaves [is] the best defense against the arm of the

---

[1] Augustus Saint-Gaudens, <u>Monument to Robert Gould Shaw and His Regiment</u>, Boston Common, Boston.
[2] Geoffrey Ward, <u>The Civil War: An Illustrated History</u> (New York: Knopf, 1990) 248.

Index